PRAISE FOR REACI

As a therapist I want you to know, this book is a treasure. If you are a person who is trans or the partner of a trans person this is a must-have book for you. I think what you'll find is a path towards hope, healing and wholeness. It's thoughtfully written and is filled with tangible help to guide you both individually and as a couple. I can't wait for you to read it!

Candice Czubernat, founder of The Christian Closet and Progressive Christian Counseling

I highly recommend this book to anyone who has a trans partner, is a trans person, a questioning person, or anyone else who is curious about how to navigate all aspects of being in a relationship with a trans person. This book is a rare and valuable resource to help facilitate the brave and honest conversations needed to manage the early days of transitioning as a couple. Written with warmth and deep insight, this guide will be a trusted companion for anyone wanting to support their transgender loved one as they navigate the path of gender transition.

Finlay Games, transmasculine YouTuber and author of *Top to Bottom*, he/him

We often wish humans came with a manual. They don't. But imagine how much more enriching our relationships could be. I have an adult transgender son and I pastor transgender people; This book is practical, transparent and groundbreaking. Suzanne has written from the pulpit of the pen and provided a way to envision healthy intimate relationships which encompass the full diversity and authenticity of each partner. Readers will grow from her insights and collections of advice as they are a balm in a Gilead of challenging circumstances. Thank you for this writing. Well done, good and faithful servant.

Rev. Dawn Bennett, Pastor Developer, The Table, Nashville, TN

Reaching for Hope *is a phenomenal resource for anyone who is transitioning, for anyone who is accompanying someone in their transition process, or even for anyone who just wants to better understand the process of transitioning into one's true self. The daily topics make this book easy to digest without overwhelming you as you go through such a difficult process. It affirms trans individuals and equips those who are helping a person transition, and it offers encouragement, grace, and acknowledgement. It helps the reader know what to expect throughout the transition process, and work through the many emotions that come up by stressing the importance of things like self-care and seeking safe resources for support. This book helped me—the cis wife of a trans person—to articulate many of my own feelings about my wife's coming out, and has given us the opportunity to better discuss and strengthen our relationship.*

Rev. Claire T. Ackleow, ELCA Pastor, Faith Lutheran Church, Jeffersonville, IN, she/they

I'm often asked by spouses of transitioning partners if I have anything to recommend to them to help them understand what their spouse is going through. Suzanne DeWitt Hall's Reaching for Hope *fills an important gap that will help both spouses navigate a transition. She does an excellent job of laying out the challenges of a transition in a relationship and tips to overcome them. I'm happy to recommend this book to anyone who asks me in the future.*

Erin Reed, transfeminine advocate, she/her

Reaching for Hope *is an essential read for anyone with a transgender loved one. While the book is focused on helping married couples much of it gives a general window of understanding into the issues a trans person faces as they reveal their true selves to their loved ones. Suzanne DeWitt Hall is honest and compassionate while also pulling no punches and mincing no words. As the pastor of a queer congregation, I will be giving this book to the families of all my trans congregants who are having trouble understanding their transition.*

Rev. Jeff Baker, Pastor of Chosen Family Church and TikTok theologian, they/them

As I began reading Reaching for Hope *my first thought was shock that a work like this, for those who love someone who is in transition, hasn't been created before. But as I read on, more and more I saw the need for a work like this. As someone who is still very new in her transition as well as someone who comes from a point of view of faith, I want to put this book in the hands of everyone I love. And even though I know many won't give it the time it deserves, I want them to have access to it. Suzanne has written so many amazing books, but with this one, she takes it up a huge level. And when you write from the heart that Suzanne has, and the love she has, it is truly life changing!*

Pastor Danielle, Trans Pastor in Louisiana

What I like about Reaching for Hope *is that it doesn't pretend to have all the answers, or to know what each couple or individual may be going through. With hands-on and lived experiences that the author has gone through, they provide suggestions and methods to relate with one's partner in ways that they had attempted. This makes the book read very genuinely and gives a non-judgmental vibe that makes the book approachable and relatable.*

I really enjoyed learning about the blue morpho butterfly in the introduction. It is a very fitting and poignant analogy of what life as a trans person can be like. This is just one example of the ways in which the author presents the information. It is an easy read and highly accessible for such a complex topic.

Jules Ackleow, UX Designer and pastor's spouse, she/they

PRAISE FOR THE WHERE TRUE LOVE IS SERIES

The church has been dreadfully behind on conversations relating to understanding and embracing our transgender and gender non-conforming siblings, and even within the LGBT+ Christian movement, there have been very few resources that are focused on the needs and experiences of this important community. Suzanne DeWitt Hall's new resource Transfigured *is changing that. This devotional is full of powerful meditations and reflections for the trans* and gender queer community as they journey deeper into their own spiritual lives and calls everyone who embarks on this forty-day journey towards a posture of radical authenticity and grounding in our truest selves. I recommend this resource for every faith community that seeks to minister well to their trans* and gender non-conforming members.*

Brandan Robertson, Lead Pastor, Missiongathering San Diego, and author of *True Inclusion: Creating Communities of Radical Embrace*

A Theology of Desire *conveys the sensual passion of spirituality and love, and their relationship. Even though we hunger for facts, finding, and fulfillment, our experience is most often questions, seeking, and desire. Suzanne beautifully expresses the beauty of this.*

David Hayword, aka 'nakedpastor', cartoonist, artist, and author of *Questions are the Answer* and other titles

I am constantly meeting people of faith who, like me, are pilgrims on the road of deconstruction. We are re-evaluating the long-held convictions we've inherited. Some of us are eager to embrace a more vibrant, inclusive, and progressive faith, but most of us just want to break free from something that feels like confinement. As freeing as this process can be, it can also be terrifying. How precious, then, to know that there are companions out there to help and support us on the journey. Suzanne DeWitt Hall is one of those companions. Her wisdom in Sleeper, Awake *is a gracious gift, offered in love, from one pilgrim to many others.*

Rev. Junia Joplin, Associate Pastor, Metropolitan Community Church of Toronto

As people of faith we must continue to unpack our sacred texts anew with every generation. Suzanne DeWitt Hall's heart beats for a Christ that is both alive and relevant in a post-Christian culture. I hope many find this book and see themselves in its words.

Timothy Kurek, author of *The Cross in the Closet*

I just finished Sex With God *and I want to read it again. The theology is consistent and grounded, linked to interesting and surprising quotes from Pope Benedict or Rainer Maria Rilke to Marilyn Monroe and Donna Summers. The theology of Sacred Sexuality opens a dialogue long held captive by the Church. How does the most intimate act we share with others reflect the intimacy of our relationship with the Divine? And how does a healthy, wholistic sexual theology better help us to understand a healthy, wholistic relationship with our God, ourselves and our world? This book begins that journey.*

Rev. Dr. Rob Apgar-Taylor, Sr. Pastor,
Grace United Church of Christ

Suzanne DeWitt Hall follows her open-hearted devotional Where True Love Is *with another collection of devotions stunning in their clarity and compassion. Her short reflections on the beauty of gender diversity—both within the spectrum of humanity, and within the self of God—offer multiple lenses for trans, genderqueer, and other non-gender-conforming people to witness their own stories in the holy books of the Christian faith. Interweaving contemporary understandings of gender with ancient biblical verses, Suzanne demonstrates how our manifold God has been continually working for the inclusion, celebration, and liberation of those too often considered "other." These forty devotions are perfect for personal meditation, or for a group study during Lent or another congregational time for self-reflection and neighborly love.*

Rev. Emmy R. Kegler, Pastor of Grace Lutheran Church,
founder of the *Queer Grace Encyclopedia*
and author of *One Coin Found*

REACHING FOR HOPE

*Strategies and support for the partners of
transgender people*

BOOKS IN THE WHERE TRUE LOVE IS DEVOTIONAL SERIES

Where True Love Is: an affirming devotional for LGBTQI+ individuals and their allies

Transfigured: a 40-day journey through scripture for gender-queer and transgender people

I Don't Want Them to Go to Hell: 50 days of encouragement for friends and families of LGBTQ people

Pro-Life, Pro-Choice, Pro-Love: 44 days of reflection for finding a third way in the abortion debate

A Theology of Desire: Meditations on intimacy, consummation, and the longing of God

Sex With God: Meditations on the sacred nature of sex in a post-purity-culture world

Sleeper, Awake: 40 days of companionship for the deconstruction process

CHILDREN'S BOOKS

Jamie the Germ Slayer

Rumplepimple

Rumplepimple Goes to Jail

REACHING FOR HOPE

*Strategies and support for the partners of
transgender people*

Suzanne DeWitt Hall

With contributions from Declan DeWitt Hall

Foreword by Fox Fisher

Cover image by fran_kie Conceptual Photography under license from Shutterstock.com

DH Strategies

First Edition
Version 1.1

ISBN-13: 978-1-7347427-5-6
Printed in the United States of America

DEDICATION

This book is for Declan, who devoted the last decade to helping me be fully myself. Now it's your turn.

Dance.

CONTENTS

FOREWORD

A very wise non-binary vicar once told me that being religious and being transgender is linked because both require faith in something which cannot fully be quantified.

I came out as trans at the end of the 20's, after many years of soul searching and trying to love myself as I was. I wanted to honour the body I was given however, it got to a point where I needed to try a medical transition, not just changing my name and pronouns.

By exploring my own gender issues, I found increasing comfort in my own skin, which, in turn, has helped me contribute so much more to the world because I finally have a place in it.

Not dealing with my gender issues and grieving the loss of some friends had resulted in making poor decisions with a partner and panic attacks like earthquakes in my body.

Trans people deserve to be believed for who they are. Being laughed at or called a fraud was my biggest fear when I was first coming out as trans to friends, family and workmates a lifetime ago, although I felt that there was nothing to lose by that point.

It's all about the little things in life, which create a sense of belonging and balance. Everyone deserves to feel safe and supported and thank goodness for pets, who love us regardless of our gender identity or physicalities. My kitten Wolfie is currently purring on my lap and his sister Fennel just brought me a feather from outside.

I'm currently in the longest, most fulfilling relationship in my life. My parents no longer worry about getting a phone call that their 'daughter' has done something drastic.

At the time of writing, we are in the midst of Trans Awareness Week, with Trans Day of Remembrance just a few days away, where we honour those who died by suicide and in horrific attacks, simply for daring to be themselves. This year, a record number of attacks on trans people was reported, so clearly the world still needs educating on what it is to be trans, and that non-binary people are not a threat to anyone else's identity as a man or a woman.

The journey for trans rights currently feels like a macabre dance, two steps forward and one step back. In one week, an actor may come out as trans, a presenter as non-binary, while in a suburb in the north of England, a young trans girl is taken away from her loving mother or a trans man and his partner, or suffer a brutal attack by a group of five men, while on their way home from a Pride event in their local seaside town.

Whether it's internalised transphobia from years of soaking up Hollywood films with subtle and not-so-subtle laughs at the expense of trans women, or a fear of something other than yourself, I hope you can make a promise to learn, to listen and to see where our similarities are.

Like life, the trans journey is never linear. A transition may never be fully 'done' and we all need to be okay with that. All people deserve to feel safe and supported. All people deserve love.

Today, I'm more 'me' than I've ever been. Identity is layers and layers of an onion skin. I know that I am more than just my body. My body is a vessel for my consciousness. Years after starting my transition, I can finally see what a gift being trans really is, despite the difficulties.

The most important thing in this world is connection, to ourselves and each other. If we don't feel seen and understood by those around us, we can feel a deep discomfort and loneliness.

By being out for the past 10 years and involved with raising awareness of trans issues by elevating trans voices, through My Genderation films; I am contacted every day by people who are wishing to support a loved one who is at the start of their transition. There's not enough support for trans allies, whether that's partners in love, work mates, friends or family members, I'm thrilled that I can now begin recommending this book.

If you're here for a human experience, you may as well get comfortable. Make steps towards your happiness and don't let anyone get in the way of that, as an act of self-love.

Stay safe, stay loved and remember that as an individual, you can make a massive difference in this world.

Fox Fisher, author of the *Trans Survival Workbook*, the *Trans Teen Survival Guide*, and other titles, he/they

---

Fox Fisher is a brown, queer, transmasculine, non-binary artist, author, filmmaker and LGBTQIA+ rights advocate. Fox co-created the *My Genderation* project, creating 100+ short films, and was awarded an Honorary Doctorate for their work on trans issues in film and other media. Fox co-founded Trans Pride, Brighton, is Advisor to All About Trans and was Artist in Residence for Homotopia Festival in 2020.

INTRODUCTION

If you're reading these words, you might be in a state of turmoil. Your beloved may have just told you they're transgender, or even handed you this book as a way to break the news.

First things first: breathe. You can get through this.

There's no denying that transitioning can be traumatic for couples. Rocky relationships may not survive. Good relationships may grow stronger. If you or your partner are determined to leave, you probably won't find this book helpful. But if you're willing to hold off on that decision, you might find that the pages offer insights and tools to give you space to think.

My spouse is transgender, and I've been writing about trans issues for years, but I'm not a psychologist. I've just walked down the road you're on and am willing to hold your hand through some of the issues you'll face. In addition to my own experience, I scoured online support groups, asked questions of trans couples, and tried to immerse myself in the situations couples go through. All our paths are different, but yours will contain some of the same mile markers.

The book is written in the style of a daily devotional, with short entries on a single topic to help you process things you might be experiencing. Reading one entry a day can be a useful way to process information slowly at a time when things feel overwhelming.

A glossary of terms is included as a crash course in terminology and for later reference. There's an index at the back so you can easily look up topics in the future. You can read it on your own or move through it with your partner if you're in a headspace which permits that.

Now that you know what the book *is*, let's talk about what it isn't:

- Medical advice.
- Psychiatric advice.
- Legal advice.
- Comprehensive of everything you and your loved one will encounter.

This thing you hold isn't perfect or all-encompassing. It's simply an attempt to help. I could probably keep adding entries forever, as new issues are revealed through my relationship with my spouse and with other trans people.

The butterfly on the back cover is a blue morpho. I chose it because it's such a lovely metaphor for transgender reality. Blue morphos aren't actually blue, but microscopic scales on their wings refract light in a way that looks blue to the human eye. Our limited human senses proclaim data about the creatures based on what we see, but their reality is something else entirely. The undersides of blue morphos are a mottled brown, designed for camouflage while resting on the ground or in trees. They look ordinary from one vantage point but have an unworldly beauty from another. When they fly they appear and disappear against the sky, their true selves peeking out and disappearing again.

Transgender people and butterflies both transform, and transformational states are fragile. Rough handling can kill them. Loving a trans person is a special calling, and not everyone can do it.

"I'm not sure if I can handle this, but I'm going to try" is a valid position, and it's good enough for where you are, in this moment.

May the words in these pages remind you that you aren't alone. Keep reaching for hope.

GLOSSARY

Terms related to gender identity and sexual orientation are morphing quickly as people increasingly discuss these issues. The definitions offered below are a starting point, but you'll probably find that usage will shift over time and within different communities.

AFAB: Acronym for *Assigned Female at Birth*. See *Sex Assignment*.

AMAB: Acronym for *Assigned Male at Birth*. See *Sex Assignment*.

Agender: An identity that doesn't align with any gender.

Bigender: An identity that aligns with both male and female genders.

Bottom Surgery: Surgical procedures that transform genitalia so that it more closely aligns with a person's gender identity.

Cisgender: A gender identity that aligns with the sex a person is assigned at birth.

Clocked/Clocking: Being recognized as transgender by a stranger.

Dead Name: The name given to a transgender person at birth that has been replaced by one which reflects their gender identity. A better phrase is *birth name*.

Dead Naming: Referring to a transgender person by their birth name.

1

Dysphoria (Gender or Body Dysphoria): Psychological distress experienced by transgender people because the image of self they see doesn't match their gender identity.

Enby: A slang term for non-binary (NB). See *Non-Binary*.

Euphoria (Gender Euphoria): Joy experienced by transgender people when the image of self they see matches their gender identity.

FTM: Acronym for *Female to Male*, referring to transmasculine people (transgender boys or men) assigned female at birth.

Femme: Gender presentation that leans toward stereotypically female concepts for clothing, hair, makeup, body language, etc.

GAS/GCS/GRS: Acronyms for *Gender Affirmation Surgery/Gender Confirmation Surgery/Gender Reassignment Surgery*. Procedures for transforming the appearance of various body parts so that they more closely align with a person's gender identity.

Gender Marker/Sex Marker: The *M*, *F*, or other designation on birth certificates, passports, licenses, etc.

Gender Expression/Gender Performance: The way a person conveys their gender through outward appearance and behavior. This can include clothing, body language, speech patterns, and other external signals.

Gender Fluid: An identity that shifts between male and female genders over time or situationally.

Hormone Therapy: Treatments in which hormone medications are administered to increase testosterone in transmasculine people and to decrease testosterone and increase estrogen in transfeminine people. Hormones contribute significantly to characteristics like genital formation, body fat distribution, hair growth patterns, and other issues. These therapies are sometimes referred to using the acronym HRT (hormone replacement therapy.)

Intersex: An umbrella term describing the sex of a person born with genitalia, hormones, or chromosome patterns that don't fit the typical definitions of female versus male.

MTF: Acronym for *Male to Female*, referring to transfeminine people (transgender girls or women) assigned male at birth.

Masc: Gender presentation that leans toward stereotypically male concepts for clothing, hair, body language, etc.

Non-Binary: An umbrella term for an identity that is neither male nor female, both male and female, or otherwise doesn't fit into the male versus female binary understanding.

Passing: When a transgender person is publicly perceived as their gender rather than the sex they were assigned at birth.

Pronouns: Parts of speech that replace proper nouns (names) when referring to people. They can be gender-binary specific (he/him/his and she/her/hers), non-specific (ze/zir/zers and others), or plural (they/them/theirs).

Sex Assignment: The gender marker you're given at birth based on an assessment of genitalia.

TERF: An acronym for Trans-Exclusionary Radical Feminist; a cisgender woman who rejects the concept of trans women being women. TERFs often work toward anti-trans legislation and exclusion of trans women from places reserved for females.

Top Surgery: Surgical procedures that transform the appearance of a person's chest so that it more closely aligns with their gender identity.

Transfeminine: Descriptor for a person who was assigned male at birth (AMAB) but whose gender identity is female. Also known as a trans woman.

Transgender: Descriptor for a person whose gender identity doesn't align with the sex they were assigned at birth. It's an umbrella term, meaning that it describes a wide spectrum of gender variance.

Transmasculine: Descriptor for a person who was assigned female at birth (AFAB) but who's gender identity is male. Also known as a trans man.

Transexual: Use of this term varies. Within the medical community, it has been used as a descriptor for transgender people who've had bodily characteristics altered to more closely align with their gender identity.

STARTING POINTS

HERE YOU ARE

Gender transition is a challenging, fearful, joyous experience for the person undertaking it, and it's a journey that ultimately can only be done by the individual themself. No one else can do it for them. The process can be isolating and alienating, leaving the trans person feeling intensely alone. You might also feel alone, particularly in the earliest days before you're able to discuss it with anyone else.

But here you are. Trying.

Not all couples can survive the turbulence which results when a person decides they can no longer live in the ill-fitting disguise of an inaccurate gender assignment. The fact that you're holding this book means you've decided to at least *try*. That says a lot about you as a person. It shows you're choosing love over fear, confusion, and pain. It shows you recognize that transition gives your loved one a chance to emerge into the world stronger, happier, and freer than they've ever been.

You've probably already experienced confusion, concern, and perhaps even shock. You might wonder if you'll be able to handle the challenges the future holds, or worry the two of you as a united entity won't hold up under the pressure.

But here you are. Trying.

How the future unfolds remains to be seen. But right now, be proud of yourself for entertaining the possibility of standing with your beloved as they strive to live authentically.

Showing up is a great gift.

Here you are. Trying.

The willingness to show up changes us. It makes us a little braver each time.
Brené Brown

6

TRANSITIONING AS A TEAM EVENT

Yesterday we talked about transition being an isolating process for the one going through it, and for you. Today we'll talk about approaching it intentionally from the perspective of teamwork.

Some people aren't surprised when their loved one reveals truth about their gender identity. Others are shocked. Sometimes we regret things we do or say in our initial reactions, when our emotions take over. If that happened in your case, there's nothing you can do other than take responsibility and try to make amends. And if you've decided that you're willing to not give up on your relationship, then it's important for both of you to recognize that it has to be a team effort. It's not possible for your partner to transition without action of some kind on your part. They're going to need support, encouragement, and a listening ear from the one with whom they're closest. And you're going to need them to perform many of those roles for you as well.

Viewing transition as a journey the two of you are undertaking together increases the likelihood your relationship will weather the challenges to come. If either of you look at it as something the other one simply needs to deal with rather than an issue to be problem solved together, the road is likely to be bumpy.

Teams can't work when the individuals within them are focused solely on themselves. They must assess how the actions of each person contribute to overall success.

It's possible that the increased authenticity of your loved one will mean your relationship will end up stronger and better than ever. But that can only happen if you're willing to work through it together.

Alone we can do so little. Together we can do so much.
Helen Keller

7

THINGS NOT TO SAY

In the early days of overwhelming emotion, it can feel like you're walking through a conversational minefield. The list of statements and questions in this section are likely to trigger conflict, and are therefore best avoided. We'll talk more about the issues they contain in the days to come.

Why are you choosing to do this?

Gender identity isn't a choice trans people make. Did you choose *your* sex and gender?

Maybe it's just a phase.

Gender is a key part of identity. It's not something people move through like a growth spurt or a design aesthetic.

Have you thought this through?

They have thought about this more than you can imagine.

Are you sure?

They're sure.

Could you just be gay?

Gender identity and sexual orientation are completely different things. Trans people can be attracted to people of the same gender or other genders. Just like cisgender people.

Why would you want to be a man?/Why would you want to be a woman?

People don't *want* to be transgender. Most fervently wish that the sex assigned at birth aligns with their gender, but unfortunately, it doesn't.

When transgender people come out to a loved one, it's not to announce that they want to change their identity. It's to say that they no longer want to pretend to be something they're not. They don't need to *become* a new gender, they already *are* that gender.

But you're so pretty!/But you're so handsome!

Trans people are exhausted from years spent playing the part of another gender and working to fit societal expectations for their appearance. Reminding them of how closely society has aligned them with the wrong gender is painful.

Does it bother you that you'll never be a *real* man?/Does it bother you that you'll never be a *real* woman?

Understandings of gender are fluid and change across time, geography, and culture. The idea that there are "real" men and "real" women is a false understanding of what gender actually is. It's hurtful to suggest that transgender people aren't "real."

Why didn't you tell me sooner?

It takes a tremendous amount of courage to push back against the force of expectations a trans person has to manage throughout their lives. Some of those expectations were probably delivered by you. Your beloved examined the countless facets of life which would be impacted by transitioning before deciding the time was right. The fact that they feel safe and brave enough to speak their truth is a testament of their courage and their hope in you.

I feel like my partner died.

You might need to speak these words somewhere as part of processing your grief, but please don't say them to your beloved. Coming out is intensely vulnerable, and they desperately need acknowledgment that their essential self is worthy of love. Using this phrase makes them feel like you loved a costume and a pretense rather than an actual person.

■ ■ ■ ■

9

Language issues will get easier as time passes. The more you learn about transgender experience, the less likely you'll be to unintentionally inflict pain.

Being transgender, like being gay, tall, short, white, black, male, or female, is another part of the human condition that makes each individual unique and something over which we have no control. We are who we are in the deepest recesses of our minds, hearts, and identities.
Linda Thompson

BELIEVE THEM

In the early days of processing the truth your loved one revealed about their gender identity, your thoughts and emotions may be wide ranging and contradictory. You might even have trouble believing what they've told you is true.

But hear this: they're not crazy.

Gender is a social construct which varies from era to era and across cultures and geography. Western understandings of masculinity and femininity don't align with those held in other places by other peoples. They vary within regions, communities, and even individual families. In every society which ascribes to the male versus female binary (not all do) trans people have always existed. Any time you try to reduce complex humanity into achromatic simplicity you're sure to find people who are brave enough to point out that they're more filled with color and nuance than that.

When your beloved shares their truth, it's an intensely vulnerable time. They're showing you great trust and asking for a lifeline. Remaining closeted makes people vulnerable to depression, drug abuse and addiction, and suicidal ideation. Transition can literally be a lifesaver.

As things move forward, the fragility typically hardens into something more resilient. In the meantime: believe them. They know how they feel, they know what they think, and they know what their lived experience has been like.

When a person says they're trans, they *are* trans. Your job is to accept that reality, and figure out how to respond.

> *I think that if there is a single thing that cis people should understand about trans people is that we aren't trans because we transition, we transition because we're trans. Stopping a trans person from transitioning doesn't make them not trans, it makes them miserable.*
> Ellie Sage

LISTEN MORE THAN YOU TALK

Imagine finding out your beloved suffered a physical or emotional injury, and you never knew about it. Let's say they'd been assaulted or were the victim of a hit and run years ago, and finally decided to talk about it. How would you handle discussions about their experience?

Chances are you'd do a lot of listening. You'd ask questions and encourage them to explore the trauma in order to reach freedom and healing. You might share some of your own experiences of things that left lingering traumatic effects, but mostly you'd probably let them talk it out.

This is exactly what transitioning people need in the early days of coming out. They need to process the various kinds of trauma that come with being expected to live gender inauthentically. They'll have experienced pain from family and friends, church communities, and the media. They'll need to grapple with the things they themselves did in order to simply keep on existing.

As the initial deluge of emotion and processing pours out, try to keep in mind the analogy of a long-standing injury, because that's really what's happened to them. Try to listen more than you talk. This can be hard because you'll go through your own phases of processing, which we'll address as you move through this book. Using a journal can be helpful as an outlet for your confusion and fear.

There will be time for you to talk, and it's important that you do. But listen first. That's your primary job initially, and it's a really, really important one.

> *When you debate a person about something that affects them more than it affects you, remember that it will take a much greater emotional toll on them than on you. For you it may feel like an academic exercise. For them, it feels like revealing their pain only to have you dismiss their experience and sometimes their humanity.*
> Sarah Maddux

DEALING WITH DECEPTION

One of our friends began hormone therapy, but her wife doesn't know she's trans. Her fear about what will happen when her spouse finds out has left her paralyzed. There's a train wreck on the horizon, and she feels helpless to prevent it.

Lying is often a fear response, and there are an overwhelming number of things for trans people to fear. Transgender people are often forced to hide truth throughout their whole lives. Many essentially lie to themselves about who they are. Some decisions aren't conscious, they're simply long-standing mechanisms for trying to survive in situations that are hostile to their very beings. Deception is a requirement for their ongoing existence.

This is a terrible reality to live under. It can take time to move out of this phase. When hiding is a survival skill, it can be hard to shake. Your loved one is brave for declaring they'll no longer submit to the suppression of their truth, because it means heading straight into a storm of fearful realities.

When a spouse finds out their loved one kept something so significant from them, it feels like a major violation of trust. You may be angry you weren't given information about your loved one's gender before agreeing to be in a committed relationship or marriage. You might even discover they've been essentially leading a double life. Your understanding of how close and truthful the two of you've been with each other may be deeply shaken.

Your pain over these things is understandable. Truthfulness is tremendously important for good relationships. Trust is foundational, and disruption of trust can be catastrophic.

But as you process these hurts, consider this:

Try to imagine what it would be like to live with such fear that you must weave a web of pretense just to be left alone. Try to envision what that would do to your heart, mind, and spirit. And try to forgive.

Your primary tool for managing the pain of feeling deceived is compassion. When your beloved experiences affirmation and support, the layers of coping mechanisms begin to fall away as the overwhelming fear is replaced by sensations of safety. This can only happen within a relationship where it's safe to be vulnerable. Creating that safe space may take intentional effort on both your parts.

This is hard, hard work. But real love *is* hard, and requires both honesty and forgiveness.

When you spend most of 40 years telling yourself it's pointless to want something because it's impossible, you cultivate a fundamental, pervasive absence of desire. You become proficient at pushing away wants because you don't trust them. And so, you become a person with no clue what she wants.
Rev. June Joplin

THEY'RE NOT DOING SOMETHING TO YOU

Humans like stability. Believing we know what's going on gives us a sense of control. When that sense of control is threatened, we tend to want to look for someone to blame.

Anger can act as a steam vent by giving overwhelming, confusing emotion somewhere to go. Because of all that, you might be tempted to view your loved one's desire to live authentically as them doing something *to* you and inflicting something *on* you.

The response is understandable but it's not accurate or fair. For transgender people, the desire to simply live as themselves without fear is a perpetual hunger. Hiding and lying about their reality is an ongoing source of internal shame. Anger, depression, abuse of alcohol or drugs in an effort to self-medicate, and other detrimental states are frequent experiences. Their coming out is not an action of violence toward your own mental health, it's a heroic attempt to protect their own.

Will there be challenges to face in this new-to-you reality? Yes. But your loved one is not your enemy, and you're not theirs. The enemy is the misunderstanding, bias, and prejudice held by so many in the world. The enemy is the absence of love. When you experience anger toward your loved one because of the wave of change headed toward your lives, remember this.

Your anger may need to burn itself out before you're able to move forward. If it doesn't dwindle, there may be deeper, interconnected causes fueling the ongoing fury. Transitioning can be the catalyst for uncovering issues which must be dealt with in order to have fulfilling, unitive, trusting, intimate relationships.

Remember: they're not doing something to you. They're doing something to save and free themselves.

I didn't transition to become someone new. I transitioned to stop hiding who I already was.
Amy Hicox

THEY AREN'T BEING SELFISH

We're entering the second week of our time together in this book, and it may seem like the focus has been entirely on your partner. This feeling may reflect what's going on in your relationship as well; your loved one may be in the throes of all kinds of emotion. They might be nearly manic with the joy of being truthful about who they are. They may be despondent about the impact the news could have on family members, friends, and work relationships. They might share frequently about dysphoria and hopes for entering into authentic gender expression, or they could be silent and brooding over it all.

The early phases of being out are frustratingly self-focused.

But they have to be.

There's a difference between temporarily centering on self and being selfish. When a person has had to deny their true selves for decades, the act of revealing and stepping into authenticity requires a specific kind of intensive energy which necessarily self-orbits. It's like the spinning of a top. A string is wound around it, creating a mass of potential energy, and when the string is zipped free, the force of the energy is released and the top spins into motion. It's not the top's fault that it bangs into things as the initial impetus is unleashed. It can't help it.

Obviously your loved one is a sentient being. They aren't a top, and are responsible for the things they say and do, regardless of the pressures they've been under.

But the action of coming out and the resulting side effect of temporary self-focus isn't selfishness. It's salvation.

Always be a first-rate version of yourself and not a second-rate
version of someone else.
Judy Garland

THIS IS NOT A REFLECTION OF YOU

I'm a complex mix of people-pleaser and don't-give-a-damn. Sometimes I carry the reactions of others on my shoulders like a heavy yoke, as if I were responsible for various unhappinesses in their lives. In other situations I easily recognize that their responses are their own problems, and disconnect from disapproval. We all reside in different places on this scale.

But let's get down to some basics. Your partner's identity has nothing to do with you. Your gender presentation didn't influence it. Your response to their past gender presentation didn't cause it. You didn't create it, and you can't change it.

If you're a people pleaser you may worry about what others are going to think about *you* when the truth comes out. You might fear they'll believe you encouraged it into being or didn't make your partner feel man or woman enough. Your thoughts about all that judgement and disapproval could go into overdrive.

The truth is it doesn't matter what other people think about you or your beloved. You aren't in control of their perceptions. What matters is figuring out what's okay and not okay for *you*. What matters is helping your partner be happy, healthy, and free.

The gender identity of your loved one is not a reflection of you. How you respond and assist them *is*.

When people begin to become their true selves, when they experience meaningful transformation, growth, or liberation, they may seem "weird" or "strange" to you now. You may not "get" them. That is OK. It's not about you.
Rev. Susan Rogers

GENDER AS A TOOL OF CONTROL

In a Vox article[1], transfeminine author Emily VanDerWerff wrote about gender being an interconnection of three ideas: gender as an innate part of the self, gender as a performance for society, and gender as a tool for dominance, hegemony, and control.

The first idea is pretty straightforward, and you've probably heard your loved one express it: they simply aren't the gender they were assigned at birth.

Gender performance refers to the ways a person conveys male or femaleness to the world, through mode of dress, speech, behavior, hair style, makeup, etc. This is also relatively straight forward. Your lo ved one may have talked to you about wanting to change gender performance characteristics as part of their transition.

The last issue is a bit more complicated but has a great deal of significance both for your situation and for society as a whole.

People who have control typically want to retain or even increase it. Politicians run for consecutive terms, dictators kill those who try to unseat them, and people who supervise others want to get promotions so they can have a wider span of control. Power dynamics within families mimic these scenarios on a smaller scale. Gender has played a huge role in dominance structures throughout history, with males and uber masculinity holding the highest position in most cultures. Hebrew and Christian scripture is filled with stories about how this plays out, and it continues in Western culture today. Women's ability to vote is a relatively recent achievement, and pay inequality, sexual assault and abuse, and lower representation in elected office are all examples of the ongoing inequity in action.

---

[1] *How Twitter can ruin a life*, Vox, June 30, 2021.

Transgender people throw a monkey wrench into this system, because without a binary it becomes much harder to draw lines of who belongs where, and therefore, who should hold control, who might be a threat to control, or who can be dismissed as essentially irrelevant.

For those interested in dismantling age-old inequitable power systems, this should be seen as a very good thing. But for a man who sees his AMAB child embracing their femininity, it can feel like a loss of the power they planned to hand down to the next generation. Similarly, transmasculine people can seem like threats to the power cisgender men have wielded throughout the centuries.

Shaking the basis of control systems is required for creating societies which demonstrate that all people have equal worth and equal rights to contribute in whatever ways their gifts lean.

People stepping out in boldness to live their authentic gender helps end unhealthy power structures. But those who are threatened with losing power aren't going to like it.

The best countries at closing the gender gap are the most peaceful.
The best countries at closing the gender gap are the most prosperous.
The most peaceful countries are the happiest. The most peaceful
countries are best on the environment.
Laurie Levin

RESPECT THEIR PRONOUNS AND NAME

Until recently, you, your family, friends, and social circles have known your loved one by the gender they were assigned at birth and the name corresponding to that gender. Requesting those people to use a chosen name and the appropriate pronouns is a significant milestone for transgender individuals. Hearing these affirming words after a lifetime of being referred to as someone they aren't is balm to an endlessly hurting wound. When people deadname a trans person or use pronouns that don't align with their gender identity, the wound is broken open again.

This can be hard for you as you try to shift your understanding of the one you love. The pattern of our thoughts is intricately connected to the words we repeat frequently, and the reverse is also true. You haven't had to think about what you call them up until now; the words simply pour out. The only time we do stop and think is when we're angry, and in that anger, we get more intentional, perhaps using their name rather than a nickname, or including their middle name. Being angry shakes us out of default. But otherwise, pronoun and name usage essentially run on autopilot.

The good news is that as your brain continues to update and expand the neural networks assigned to knowledge of your loved one, it will get increasingly easier. Eventually, the pronouns and name that feel awkward replace what came before and are transformed into the new normal.

Starting Points

Your emotions about the deeper ramifications of these language changes are real and valid, and we'll talk about them as we move together through this book. The pain some partners feel about a name change is specifically discussed in the *Your Emotions Are Valid* section. But please don't underestimate the importance of a name and pronouns to your loved one. Names hold great power. Your handling of theirs can bring joy, or crush their spirit.

Life is not a matter of creating a special name for ourselves, but of uncovering the name we've always had.
Richard Rohr

TURNING AROUND IS HARD

As you contemplate the challenges of transitioning and worry about the disruption it could mean for your lives, the fear and apprehension can feel overwhelming for both of you. Your level of discomfort may get so intense that you can't help but wish your loved one could just return to their previous state of hiddenness. You might think that if they'd simply do that, all the disruption and confusion would disappear, and life would return to the stasis you previously considered normal.

But the life before your loved one revealed their truth wasn't experienced by them the way it was by you. For them, the storm had been brewing and growing until the atmospheric pressure of dysphoria, denial, and deceit became unbearable. The blue skies you saw were simply an illusion.

It's hard for trans people to go back into hiding. The taste of freedom and authenticity is heady. For many, it's not possible to go back to an existence of shame, deception, and discomfort, even though they recognize that life will be a new kind of difficult.

Most people don't like to hide truth or deceive others. All people want to be accepted for who they are. Turning back to living that way is often simply not possible.

Freedom is the open window through which pours the sunlight of the human spirit and human dignity.
Herbert Hoover

YOU'RE GOING TO NEED TO TALK

Walking through transition with your partner is as much of a journey for you as it is for them. If they seek gender affirmation options through healthcare, counseling is often included. Optimally you'll also seek counseling together to help work through issues as they come up. You may want to get counseling independently as well if that's an option for your schedule and your finances[2]. But there are a lot of hours outside counseling sessions when your mind may whirl with questions and emotions.

It's important to remember that stepping into the truth of gender identity isn't about you, it's about your loved one. The role of being the most intimate companion to them is a tender responsibility. Controlling the language you use and the emotion you display to them, particularly in the early days, will have a big impact on the future health of your relationship. When we say things in the heat of an emotional moment, we often speak without measuring the impact, and the resulting scars can be long-lasting. You'll need to process your thoughts and feelings and should have someone to talk to other than your beloved, so you can vent in a way that doesn't need to be filtered. Sometimes we simply need to state things so we can hear them out loud and assess what we really, rationally, think about them.

Finding this person can be a challenge in situations when you, your partner, or your family is not yet ready to go public. If this is the case for you, consider talking with your partner about identifying one person who will guard the information while permitting you to have a place to let off steam. Hopefully there's someone you're both comfortable with in that role. If that's simply not possible, confidential support groups for partners of trans people on social media can provide an outlet for your concerns. They're also a great source of collective wisdom.

---

[2] Potential counseling resources are listed in Appendix A.

In the meantime, journaling can help. The act of simply writing our thoughts down acts like a pressure release valve, and helps you figure out which issues need to be raised with your loved one and which don't.

It's natural to need to talk. Setting yourself up to do so helps both you and your loved one.

I know a lot of people think therapy is about sitting around staring at your own navel—but it's staring at your own navel with a goal. And the goal is to one day to see the world in a better way and treat your loved ones with more kindness and have more to give.
Hugh Laurie

TAKE CARE OF YOUR PHYSICAL BEING

It's important to remember to take care of yourself. Drink plenty of water. Take your meds and vitamins. Cry. Do something physical to release cortisol, a stress hormone that causes all sorts of physical problems when accumulated at elevated levels for extended periods.

Perhaps hardest of all: get some sleep.

Stress and anxiety cause sleep disruption, and without sleep we aren't as equipped to manage our emotions. Transitioning yourself to acceptance of your loved one's reality requires you to be as in control of your emotions as possible, and getting enough sleep plays a critical role in being able to do that.

It's unreasonable to expect solid sleep every night, but you'll need decent rest at least some of the time. And this isn't solely so that you can help your partner; it permits you to problem solve and simply function through the demands of daily life. Sleep is self-care.

Meditation techniques, relaxation routines, sleep apps, bedtime stories designed for adults, and chamomile tea can all help. If you don't have health issues that prevent them, natural sleep aids like melatonin are useful. If none of these things work, talk to your doctor to see if medication is called for.

The earth will continue spinning long after the shock of all this wears off, after the two of you have resolved how to move forward, and even after you've both merged into the stuff of dirt and stars. There will be bad days and good ones. You will laugh, and love, and make a difference to those around you.

Take care of your body, even if you don't feel remotely interested in doing so right now. You've got a lot to offer our hurting world, and to the people who love you.

Go out for a walk. It doesn't have to be a romantic walk in the park, spring at its most spectacular moment, flowers and smells and outstanding poetical imagery smoothly transferring you into another world. It doesn't have to be a walk during which you'll have multiple life epiphanies and discover meanings no other brain ever managed to encounter. Do not be afraid of spending quality time by yourself. Find meaning or don't find meaning but 'steal' some time and give it freely and exclusively to your own self. Opt for privacy and solitude. That doesn't make you antisocial or cause you to reject the rest of the world. But you need to breathe. And you need to be.

Albert Camus

YOU'RE GOING TO SCREW UP

Despite having the best of intentions, you're going to use the wrong pronoun or name, make a joke that might have flown previously but falls flat in your new reality, or melt down and say things you shouldn't. None of us is perfect.

For minor flubs, don't make a big deal out of it because it can cause even more pain. But don't dismiss or defend your screw ups either. Simply acknowledge that it happened and move on. For example, if you use the wrong pronoun, just say, "Sorry, I meant <correct pronoun>." If you use the wrong name, simply correct it immediately, and continue on with your statement, question, or thought. Handling it this way lets your loved one know you're respectful of their identity and working to adjust your habits, which hopefully minimizes their discomfort.

Sometimes the mistakes will be larger than misspeaking. You might have a bad day and vent to your loved one in hurtful ways. When this happens, take ownership of what you said or did. Acknowledge that you understand why it hurt them. Explain that you're working through your own transformation and that some days things just feel overwhelming. Then think about what you'll do next time to avoid hurting them, and tell them that plan.

We're human. Screw ups are inevitable, especially during times of high emotion and change. The early days of a loved one's coming out are filled with both, so have compassion on yourself.

We all mess up. What matters is how we handle it afterward.

We are all damaged. We have all been hurt. We have all had to learn painful lessons. We are all recovering from some mistake, loss, betrayal, abuse, injustice or misfortune. All of life is a process of recovery that never ends. We each must find ways to accept and move through the pain and to pick ourselves back up. For each pang of grief, depression, doubt or despair there is an inverse toward renewal coming to you in time. Each tragedy is an announcement that some good will indeed come in time. Be patient with yourself.
Bryant McGill

YOUR EMOTIONS ARE VALID

FEELING OVERWHELMED

Your loved one has most likely spent a long time considering what it means to be transgender before deciding to be open with you. In addition to living it, they've probably also done a significant amount of research. When they can finally talk freely, it might feel like an avalanche of information, with unfamiliar terms and concepts which sound like a foreign language. And that's just the information side of things.

There may also be a landslide of decision-making about who to tell and when, how to handle things at work, communication with children, and many other issues, all of which are borne along by a virtual tsunami of emotion.

We'll talk about various kinds of emotions you may experience over the next several days, but the bottom line is you'll probably have times when you feel overwhelmed by the whole thing, and that's natural. It doesn't make you a bad person; it makes you human.

You may need to take timeouts from discussions and simply give your mind, body, and spirit space to breathe. Go out into the sunshine. Get some exercise to clear your head and free your body from stress-induced high cortisol levels. Do the things you normally do for relaxation and pleasure.

If feeling overwhelmed becomes your default state, try scheduling time when you intentionally don't think about or discuss transition issues. Scheduling selfcare increases your ability to be as rational as possible.

Courage doesn't happen when you have all the answers. It happens when you are ready to face the questions you have been avoiding your whole life.
Shannon L. Alder

FEELING SCARED

There are a lot of things to worry about when your beloved comes out as transgender: how family members will receive the news, whether your relationship can survive, what your church community will think, whether your partner will be safe, and many more issues.

Fear is a useful evolutionary trait that drives us to protective action when threats are present. It keeps us alive and safe. But as with any good and useful thing, it can become more powerful than is helpful or healthy. Fear can propel us forward, but it can also leave us frozen and unable to process information in order to make effective decisions.

If you're struggling with fear, here are a few things that can help:

- Don't try to stuff it down or pretend it isn't there.

- Remind yourself that fear is simply an emotion. Try to examine it objectively, as if someone else were experiencing it, and imagine advising them about how to respond. This can give you a bit of emotional distance to help clarify your thinking.

- Understand what you can and can't control. For example, you *can* control your words and actions, but you *can't* control the responses of others. Fear can make us feel like we're helpless, but we're not. For things over which you've got control, you can develop plans for how to minimize negative outcomes. For things you can't control, consciously release them by envisioning them leaving your grip as you uncurl your fists.

- Think longer term. Instead of focusing on all the immediate stuff that triggers fear, consider how your relationship might look when your partner is more fully themselves a year down the road. Or three years.

- Educate yourself. Fear is often triggered by unknowns, so learning more about scary things can help reduce it. You're educating yourself right now. Good job!

- Seek success stories from people who've overcome the things that trigger your fears. Hearing how others were successful combats the fear, and teaches you useful strategies.

- Visualize success. Our brains are fascinating, changeable things. When we envision positive outcomes, the neural networks for positive thought are strengthened and solidified. Visualizing successes for things you fear helps your brain create mental maps for overcoming them.

- Practice mindfulness. Be right where you are, moment by moment. This is a good spiritual practice for life as a whole, but it's particularly important during times of stress. Enjoy the small things; the taste of your morning coffee or tea, the sound of birds chirping, the fresh scent of cut grass, the feel of your beloved's hand on your back. Life is composed of individual moments, and the only control we have over reality is during each single point in time. So linger there.

Fear is a normal response to unknowns. It's useful for our emotions to inform our actions, but they shouldn't drive them. Don't let fear control you.

You encounter God in the stranger that you fear.
Rev. Joshua Noah

FEELING GUILTY

When you love someone, you want what's best for them, and you want them to be happy. These two things can feel like they're in conflict when considering the reality that trans people face. The desire to protect your beloved may seem counter to your hope that they'll feel complete.

This complex mix can make you feel guilty, and it's not the only thing that does. Speaking in a way that hurts your partner can make you feel guilty. Not wanting your life turned upside down can make you feel guilty. Talking to other people about your feelings can make you feel guilty.

Transition can be compared to the process plants go through in order to produce fruit. First there is a bud, that bursts into flower. You might really, truly, deeply love the flower, but it's simply part of what's to come. The flower withers, the bud at its base swells, change happens, and eventually an apple, quince, or pomegranate ripens. You can be happy the fruit is now whole, fragrant, and fully formed. And you can be sad that the flower you enjoyed so much is no longer there.

You don't need to feel guilty about missing the flower. You just can't get stuck there.

Chronic remorse, as all the moralists are agreed, is a most undesirable sentiment. If you have behaved badly, repent, make what amends you can and address yourself to the task of behaving better next time. On no account brood over your wrongdoing. Rolling in the muck is not the best way of getting clean.
Aldous Huxley

FEELING EMBARRASSED

There are many paths leading to where you are today. Each path equips you for responding to your loved one's transition differently. Some people are part of the LGBTQIA+ community and very familiar with transgender issues. Others are allies, and have some familiarity. Some have trans acquaintances but don't know anything about trans identity. Still others are ensconced in socially conservative circles with zero information on the subject other than what has been taught by faith communities and political news. Our personalities are all different as well. We each apply differing values to the thoughts and impressions of others.

Where you are in this multitude of pathways determines how much embarrassment you're likely to feel about the reality that your loved one is transgender.

As with fear, the first thing to do is acknowledge that it's happening. Sublimating its existence simply creates a shadow entity that makes its way out in unhealthy ways.

You can't control the thoughts and reactions of others. You can only control your own behaviors. If embarrassment is a challenge for you, try to think about how you'll behave in triggering situations. It's important to remember that you're not what other people think of you, and your loved one is not what other people think they are. You're both yourselves, in all your perfect imperfection and unique beauty. The idea that other people should have a say or feel superior over anyone else's identity is laughable.

If you're really struggling with embarrassment, you might need to discuss the issue with a counselor. It's possible that some old woundedness is coming to light, which can permit you to achieve healing and freedom. You deserve both.

> *While we can't instantly stop ourselves from getting startled or from feeling fear in response to the things that scare us, we do have the power to change how we relate to these emotions, which is all that counts. The more we learn to welcome our fear and anxiety, work with them, and weave them into the lives we want to lead, the less beholden we are to the whims of the amygdala [the brain's fear control center]. And eventually, with enough effort and patience, the conscious mind gains the power to say, "Hey, amygdala, I've got this one under control."*
> Taylor Clark

FEELING EXCLUDED

Transitioning is a bit like being in a new relationship, except with yourself. The process of discovery is seductive, scary, and consuming. Just as two people in the early stages of love are enraptured with each other to the point of neglecting other aspects of their world, trans people are in the process of falling in love with their true selves, for the first time, and may be similarly enchanted in ways that can make their partners feel excluded.

If your original reaction to the news of your partner's true gender was less than optimal, the exclusion can be more extreme. They might feel like they need to shield you from the discomfort of talking about it or participating in decision making. They may also feel like they need to protect themselves from the pain of ongoing negativity. In this situation, the best thing to do is acknowledge that your initial reaction was hurtful, but that you're actively working on learning how to be supportive.

And then be supportive.

Regardless of how you initially responded, the best hope for dealing with feelings of exclusion is by finding ways to be included. Listen actively by maintaining eye contact, asking questions, and summarizing what you think you heard at the end of a conversation. Invite your partner to engage in activities commonly associated with their gender. Ask to go with them when they shop for clothes or other items which align with their identity. Consider how you can help.

It might be painful to participate in some of these activities, but the alternative is to be excluded. You'll need to decide which kind of discomfort you prefer.

If your loved one truly *is* excluding you and you aren't sure why, the first step is to ask, and let them know you want to be part of their blossoming (if you *do* want that). In relationships with effective communication systems, they should be able to respond. If your relationship has a history of communication difficulty, you might need the help of a counselor to break through and heal the root causes.

I woke up with the love of my life standing before me—with eyes bright enough to light up the entire midnight sky, a heart strong enough to hold even the darkest of souls, and a love that had the ability to bring smiles to the world around her. I woke up today with the love of my life standing before me—and she...was me.
Samantha Gabardi

FEELING REJECTED

People in transition fall in love with becoming authentic, but through that process there's a former persona who isn't quite so easy to leave behind. Transitioning people go through something like divorce with the person they enacted while living in the sex assigned at birth. And divorce is messy. Problems crop up that you don't expect. The things you leave behind can cause grief. And when the person you love is divorcing the person you thought you married, feelings of rejection are understandable. If they reject that beloved being, are they also rejecting you?

In some cases, the answer may be yes. If they married you as part of their gender cover, they may not want to remain married. In these situations, you may experience actual rejection.

The hard reality is that a transgender person's decision to live authentically is *their* journey. In optimal situations, their partner is invited along for the ride and the two can work out how to move forward in the best possible way together. But our realities are often less than optimal, and the stressors of transition can cause further fracturing. If you haven't been able to be supportive, your beloved may push you away.

If you're dealing with more subtle forms of feeling rejected, you'll need to find ways to communicate your vulnerability with your beloved without shutting them down in self-protection. Talking it through with your trusted outside listener can help you reach the stage where you can do that. If you're seeing a counselor, they can also help you form sentences that are less likely to trigger pain and deepen the distance you're already feeling.

Your partner is in charge of charting the course of their transition. You're in charge of charting how you respond. The love you share will hopefully carry you through phases in which you feel the pain of rejection. But it may not, and if not, you're still needed in the world and have a great deal to offer. Their rejection isn't a measure of your value.

> *Everyone says love hurts, but that is not true. Loneliness hurts.*
> *Rejection hurts. Losing someone hurts. Envy hurts. Everyone gets*
> *these things confused with love, but in reality love is the only thing in*
> *this world that covers up all pain and makes someone feel wonderful*
> *again. Love is the only thing in this world that does not hurt.*
> Meša Selimović

FEELING IRRITATED

There's a good chance you'll find yourself irritated as the transition process unfolds, even if you've been 100% behind it from the beginning. Your loved one may debate about an action for what feels like eternity, and then suddenly make a move. They may change their mind a lot. They might shift back and forth between joy and fear. They might exclude you.

And then there are small things. Your partner may try out new ways of speaking or behaving that you find confusing or alarming. Trans men may test new ways of expressing sexual desire, anger, protectiveness, or other emotions to match a particular style of masculinity. Trans women may experiment with the use of voice, body movement, and dress associated with a particular style of femininity. Your partner might borrow something that has been exclusive to your use until now; a razor or a piece of clothing.

You'll be experimenting too as you try to figure out how to engage with this person you knew and yet did not know. You'll be irritating in your attempts at humor, or your use of new endearments, or your reaction when they try on your favorite pants.

There isn't much you can do to avoid irritation with uncertainty. But you can and should set boundaries around object use. Discussing rules for razors can save a lot of arguments.

Annoyances are bound to happen. Both of you will need to extend grace as you navigate the new, evolving normal.

After all, if all gender is on some level a performance (and it is), then it can be co-opted and perverted by the state. But if it's also innate on some level (and it is), then we're powerless against whatever it is that enough people decide gender performance should look like. We're constantly trapped by gender, even when we know we're trapped by it. You can't truly escape something so all-pervasive; you can only negotiate your own terms with it, and everybody's terms are different.
Emily VanDerWerff

FEELING LIKE A HYPOCRITE

Being in a relationship with a closeted transgender person happens in couples of deep faith in a divine source of love and light, and to atheists; to conservatives and progressives; to old and young. You may have considered yourself a "death-to-us-part" kind of person, pledged to see your beloved through the worst imaginable circumstances, and are now considering leaving the relationship because you simply can't accept the shifts underway. Or you may have been a long-standing ally of the LGBTQIA+ community, committed to working toward inclusion, affirmation, equality, and justice, but are reeling from the challenge of accepting that your loved one has been part of it all along.

These kinds of situations (and others) can make you feel like a hypocrite. The complexity of emotions you're currently managing might seem like they don't align with the intellectual commitments you've made in the past.

In moral psychology, hypocrisy is defined as the failure to follow one's own expressed rules and ethical principles. But the root word comes from a Greek term related to acting, or "playing a part." Acknowledging that your reaction isn't in line with your principles can be helpful in moving you to the next stage in your own transition process. Your level of commitment to ideals is being tested in a particular way. Have you been merely playing a part?

Responses to feeling like a hypocrite can take a few paths. You can simply ignore it and hope it goes away, or you can realize that you need to redefine the validity and extent of those convictions given the reality of your experiences.

None of these responses makes you a bad person. You're on a journey, just as your partner is. You've been given the opportunity to learn about yourself and decide what you want love to look like. It's time to assess your relationship and determine whether it's strong enough to withstand the current storm.

Feeling hypocritical offers you the opportunity to face deep truths. This is your life. Be the person you want to be.

All of us are put in boxes by our family, by our religion, by our society, our moment in history, even our own bodies. Some people have the courage to break free.
Geen Rocero

FEELING INVISIBLE

Your partner might have a supportive circle that tells them how courageous they are for pushing through the consuming challenges of transition. If they do, that's fantastic! But it can add to your sense of lost identity if you don't have cheerleaders telling you you're awesome too. Feeling like you don't matter or are becoming invisible is a natural response in this situation.

In the early days, there might not be a lot you can do about this. We all have seasons in our lives in which we're absorbed by significant events; job changes, the illness or death of loved ones, the birth of children, retirement, etc. It's part of the natural pattern for couples to have times of greater and lesser ability to be thoughtful. Transition is one of these times, and your role for a while may be to simply be patient in waiting it out.

That's not to say you can't try to make it better. There's nothing wrong with telling your loved one you need their attention, affection, and affirmation. If you're generally supportive of your partner's process, they'll hopefully recognize that some things need to be about you rather than them. If they love you, they'll want to respond. If they consistently can't, there are potentially issues needing mediation in a counseling setting.

Your beloved's transition and authenticity are hugely important, but your life is important too. You deserve to be seen, supported, and loved.

In the hero stories, the call to go on a journey takes the form of a loss, an error, a wound, an unexplainable longing, or a sense of a mission. When any of these happens to us, we are being summoned to make a transition. It will always mean leaving something behind...The paradox here is that loss is a path to gain.
David Richo

FEELING PAIN ABOUT A NAME CHANGE

Names are deep and powerful things. We're not always crazy about the ones our parents give us, and for transgender people, gendered name assignments are often downright painful. As your loved one moves forward in transition, they're likely to choose a name to fit their identity. This change can be painful for you. And even though there is excitement in using a name that reflects who they are, letting go of a gendered name can be painful for a trans person too, especially when it was given in honor of a grandparent or other cherished family member.

Pain associated with the name change of your loved one often relates to its connection to memories. If you dated as teenagers, you may have written your names entwined in a heart or carved them on a tree. You might recall moments when seeing their name appear on your phone made your heart go pit-a-pat. You might have a wedding gift inscribed with your names. Your children's birth certificates include them. All of these things are touchstones of how your relationship progressed, so it's logical to feel pain associated with the shift.

Nicknames can carry similar emotional weight.

To manage that pain, it can be helpful to remember that the events occurred with the person themselves, in all their extravagant detail. They happened with the wholeness of your beloved: the way they embraced and loved, the way they worried and suffered, the way they snored and laughed. Your memories aren't really about the name you were used to calling them. That person is still with you. Those experiences remain. The new name is simply a better manifestation of their true wholeness, and an opportunity to give them the gift of acknowledgement and understanding.

It can take a bit of practice and self-correction, but you'll grow used to their chosen name. You'll come up with new nicknames that better reflect the truth of their being and establish new memories and touchstones using this truer reflection.

Name changes can hurt. But you'll be okay.

There's power in naming yourself, in proclaiming to the world that this is who you are. Wielding this power is often a difficult step for many transgender people because it's also a very visible one.
Janet Mock

NOT WANTING TO HURT ANYONE

Transitioning is going to upset folks. It's hard to exist in our era without knowing at least a handful of people who don't understand the complexity of gender identity and sexual orientation. The reality is that your beloved, and you by extension, are going to have to face people's disapproval, confusion, and even pain. This issue is particularly challenging for people-pleasers and empaths: those who pick up the emotions and reactions of others.

Through this discomfort, you're being offered an opportunity for your own freedom and growth. It's an invitation to internalize the fact that you're not responsible for the responses of other people. You can help with their education and learning how to interact with your beloved in ways that don't induce dysphoria or pain. You can pray for them if you're the praying type. But beyond that, their responses are their own issue.

If you're a people pleaser, it's time to do some growing. You've got a lot on your plate just by being there for your loved one and trying to manage your own confusion. To protect your emotional health, you need to find ways to release your worry about people feeling hurt.

Each person in your circle of family and friends has the chance to learn and grow through your partner's bravery. Don't let your protectiveness get in the way of that growth.

I dare to dream of a world where people can dress, speak, and behave how they want, free from mockery, derision, judgment, harassment, and danger. This is what I want. Who's with me?
Juno Dawson

ANALYZING YOUR EMOTIONS

In order to effectively problem solve what's going on when friction arises, you need to understand what it is you're actually feeling in the moment.

Are you hurt that you're being left out? Are you angry at a particular choice or action? Are you frightened of a potential future event? Are you resentful that there's so much focus on your partner? Are you irritated by changes in behavior?

What's happening internally isn't always obvious, which means you might need a moment to evaluate. Taking timeouts can help with this. Stepping away for a bit is a useful tool for de-escalating emotion and improving communication.

The best way to start employing this technique is by agreeing to it ahead of time. If you simply withdraw when something triggers a negative response, your partner may think you're acting out of anger and using that anger against them. Set simple ground rules for how it can work; when you'll both check back in, how you'll follow up, etc.

It can be hard for some people to withdraw when emotion is high. This is particularly true for those who tend to want to fix things immediately. Training yourselves to realize time for reflection is helpful and not just a delay tactic may be necessary.

A critical piece of the time-out technique is that you've got to follow up once the reflection period wraps up. You can't just ghost the conversation and not return. This leads to distrust of the process, which doesn't do anyone any good.

Your emotions are valid, and important, and so are your beloved's. It's not always easy to recognize what's actually occurring. Getting to the bottom of what's happening in your heart and mind is the only way to work on making things better.

The pain trans people experience isn't because of who they are. It's because of the way the world is.
Declan DeWitt Hall

GAINING STRENGTH THROUGH THE PROCESS

You may never have expected to need patience the way you need it now. But as you move through the exacting early days of transitioning and emerge into a space where it's no longer new, you'll probably discover you're made of stronger stuff than you realized.

Transition isn't a sprint, it's a marathon. And it isn't linear, it's a web of movement that jumps forward and then twists back on itself. Give yourself patience and space. So much of what you're both going through is new, and you'll need emotional time and room to expand.

Athletes only get better through practice. Endurance is only built through ongoing work. The easy things in life don't create growth; it's the challenges that push our boundaries and make us stretch.

Your soul is stretching.

The things you're going through right now might not be easy, but the eventual rewards will be worth it. You're growing and strengthening in ways you couldn't have imagined. Take a deep breath and just pause for a moment to be proud of yourself.

I grabbed hold of pain with both hands and all of my heart, allowing it to shake my insides, ridding me of all that was not meant to be there, and I've become beautiful for it. I'm thankful.
Samantha Gabardi

THINGS THEY'LL EXPERIENCE

EACH SITUATION IS UNIQUE

"There is no single transgender experience" is a refrain you'll hear repeatedly as you turn these pages. Each person and couple is unique. Each comes with a particular set of strengths, challenges, desires, and vulnerabilities.

Some trans people are fulfilled simply by expressing gender in a way that feels natural and are comfortable with their external sex characteristics. Others find their bodies deeply troubling and seek gender confirmation therapies and surgeries. Some come out to the world, change their name, and restart life as their authentic selves. Others don't change anything except telling you who they really are. Some are highly sensitive to being misgendered or deadnamed. Others don't find it quite as triggering.

Gender presentation preferences are also wide ranging. Some trans women like long hair, makeup, dresses, and heels, others prefer short hair, jeans, and flannel shirts. Trans men can go full on lumberjack or prefer highly tailored clothes in fine fabrics with floral details. There is no "correct" way to be trans.

We'll talk about a number of these issues in greater detail later in this book. For now, it's enough to recognize and remember that even if you know a whole bunch of transgender people, the experiences they've described may not match what your partner and you go through.

Comparing ourselves to others isn't useful. Embracing the uniqueness of your particular situation helps you problem-solve the issues you both face in the most effective way possible.

You are who you are because you're called to be that.
Rev. Dawn Bennett

FOUNDATIONAL DISRUPTION

Maslow's Hierarchy of Needs is a psychological development theory describing the way humans grow emotionally. It's often illustrated as a pyramid, like the one below:

The essential premise is that each stage can't be fully entered unless the stage beneath it is fulfilled. The first stage is having basic needs met; food, clothing, housing, etc. Without those things, the second stage is hard to accomplish, because you can't feel safe if you're hungry and shivering. Once your basic needs are met and you feel secure, the ability to love and accept love can be realized. Without mastering the love stage, it's hard to achieve self-esteem, and feel like you're respected. And if that whole structure isn't in place, you aren't able to dance into your giftings and bring light and life to the world.

---

[3] "Maslow's hierarchy of needs" by Alexfilip96 is licensed under the Creative Commons Attribution-Share Alike 4.0 International license.

Transgender people often don't fully experience the safety, belonging, and self-esteem phases while trying to live as the gender assigned at birth. Functioning within a system of unmet needs has an impact on many aspects of life.

When a person comes out, this chart can be turned upside down. Some people experience homelessness due to the extremity of reaction by family members, which means the most foundational of all needs is stripped away. Trans people often feel unsafe, they worry about the loss of love and acceptance by those closest to them, they fear they don't fit in anywhere, and they think they're losing the respect of others.

The way you function as a couple is unique to the two of you. Working your way through transition with your loved one might be easy or excruciating. But regardless of your individual circumstances, hopefully you can give some thought to the kinds of disruption your beloved experienced during their emotional development, and what kinds they are experiencing now. Doing so helps provide a framework for understanding their responses as the process unfolds.

One can choose to go back toward safety or forward toward growth.
Growth must be chosen again and again; fear must be overcome
again and again.
Abraham H. Maslow

ROLLER COASTER EMOTIONS

Transitioning people often ride an emotional rollercoaster; one moment they're filled with jubilation at being free to talk about their reality and experiment with that newfound freedom, the next moment they're consumed with despair about the potential reaction of the world, and the impact on loved ones. They may feel jealous of cisgender people, and even of you. They may be rocked by dysphoria, or mourn the years lost. There are likely to be ups and downs that shift dramatically from day to day, especially in the early phases.

Hormone therapy can contribute to mood shifts. Testosterone may cause anger spikes or flatten emotions. Many report that this lessens with time. Estrogen may result in a greater degree of nuance and breadth of emotion than previously experienced, and your loved one may feel things more deeply and cry more easily. Communicating about the timing of doses can help you hold emotional space for them at times in the cycle when they tend to have trouble.

If and when your loved one enters into counseling, they may be urged to do the hard work of facing long-repressed trauma. Doing so can unleash a torrent of emotion, and can even halt the transition process. Here's how transgender author Torrey Peters describes one aspect of what transitioning people go through:

> *The awful part was watching what therapy called "your coping mechanisms" flame out. There was a moment in which you could catch a glimpse of how scared you'd been and the degree of pain in which you'd been living as a boy, before that pain and fear actually hit you and shredded you.... And then you developed new coping mechanisms, new language, new walls to keep yourself safe.... It was overwhelming.*[4]

---

[4] *Detransition, Baby*, Serpent's Tail/Profile Books Limited, January 2021

Things They'll Experience

In adolescence we all tend to experience this rollercoaster of highs and lows. We're given expanding levels of freedom to move around and test the new space, and that freedom is both exhilarating and terrifying. We find the world, our families, and even ourselves aren't quite as ready as we thought for the unfurling of wings that inevitably knock things around and shock us with the power of transformation.

You might find yourself moving forward and backward with your own emotional responses, acceptance, and concern. The *Tangible Helpfulness* section of this book offers some things to do to keep both of your attitudes positive.

The best advice I can offer is to try to go with the flow, to ride with the waves rather than fight them. And to take care of yourself.

In trans women's eyes, I see a wisdom that can only come from having to fight for your right to be recognized as female, a raw strength that only comes from unabashedly asserting your right to be feminine in an inhospitable world.
Julia Serano

THEY'RE GOING TO NEED TO TALK

Transitioning people need to talk things through in order to process their experience. Your partner may be seeing a counselor, so they have a good outlet for working through questions once a week. Meanwhile, there are six days and a lot of hours spent trapped in their brains with all their questions, hopes, and concerns. And if your partner isn't in counseling, they don't even have that hour.

Transition is a process of unfolding, and some issues will be revisited repeatedly. Online support groups can help, but there will be plenty of times when talking to you is the best or only option.

Here are a few suggestions from other partners of trans people:

- Try to listen deeply and hear their words with your mind, heart, and body.

- Think carefully before speaking.

- Encourage your beloved to let you know if they don't like the way you're asking questions or making statements, so you can adjust how you approach issues.

There may be moments when you're emotionally tapped and simply can't handle a discussion. Setting up systems for conversation can help. For example, if talking at night means you'll be awake for hours thinking or worrying, agreeing to talk earlier in the day makes sense. If talking about it every day is too much, then agree on a schedule and plan ways to capture thoughts and questions for those scheduled conversations. Regardless of the system, make sure you follow through. Knowing there will be a time and place to talk can take the pressure off your loved one who might feel like they're boiling over.

Trans people need to talk. If it can't be with you, it's still needed. Recognizing and supporting the importance of having an outlet is crucial for the health of you both.

I wouldn't be where I'm today without friends who could see me. Friends who have seen me. Not for who I was, not for the past and all those conventions and expectations. But for my potential. For who I was becoming. For what God was creating with me.
Rev. Junia Joplin

THEIR UNDERSTANDING OF SELF MIGHT SHIFT

My spouse Declan posed the following questions on several social media platforms:

"What is a man? What is a woman?"

These seem like simple questions, yet people struggled to answer. No one responded by simply listing genitalia, and that's a very good thing. Recognizing that masculinity and femininity are not definable by external sex characteristics alone leaves much more room for trans experience to be acknowledged, accepted, and even celebrated.

Your loved one has lived a life in the gender assigned to them, which created an in-between state of being. But most of us have been conditioned to believe in a binary male-versus-female system where in-betweens are dismissed. Humans don't like complexity and nuance, and so we create endless categories of black and white into which we can slot things and people. But the realities of the world are much more colorful.

As your beloved explores the reality of their being, their views about how they want to exist within the world may shift. They might end up falling into typical gender performance and identity, or they may conclude they're somewhere in the hazy shifting between colors, like in the spectrum of light in a rainbow. Non-binary, agender, genderfluid, and other variations are real identities, and are all authentic ways to live and express our unique realities.

Things They'll Experience

Transition is a process and an exploration of self, and explorations often reveal unexpected things. The destination is not certain and isn't the point. The journey of discovery is where growth happens.

Deciding to transition doesn't mean you have your gender, sexuality, or even who you are as a person completely figured out. It just means you know where you are isn't working and which direction you need to go to even have a chance at figuring it out. It's ok to be confused.
Twitter account @k_tea_cat

DYSPHORIA

Dysphoria is the emotional distress experienced by transgender people due to the mismatch of their physical being and their gender identity. Numerous body image issues can be dysphoria triggers, including the presence or absence of facial and body hair, menstruation, genitalia, voice, and musculature. Dysphoria can also be triggered by things like being misgendered, looking at old photos, dealing with bureaucracy that demands use of a deadname, or interacting with family members who can't or won't acknowledge your loved one's gender identity.

It can be very hard to separate whether dysphoria is caused by inherent internal states or social expectations. As life unfolds from childhood to adulthood, the two become so intertwined it can be impossible to separate them.

Avoiding dysphoria completely is probably impossible, but if you pay attention to what the triggers are, you may be able to reduce the frequency or degree of disruption by thinking creatively. For example, if your loved one manages the paperwork for your household, you could take on that task until a name change is completed and rolled out through the various places that require it. One trans woman experienced significant dysphoria when she saw herself without a wig. There were mirrors on the bedroom closet doors, so her dysphoria was triggered every morning when she woke up. To prevent this, her partner hung curtains in front of the doors so the mirrors could be used when needed but weren't visible at times when her beloved didn't want to see them.

Trans people experience phases of greater and lesser pain about not looking, sounding, or otherwise presenting the way cisgender people do. Reaching a stage of acceptance about the limits of change for their particular situation is an essential part of the transition journey. There will be joys about some changes and frustration about things that can't shift. Focusing on the things that can be achieved rather than those that can't is helpful, as are mindfulness practices.

Hopefully a day will come when they realize that being the particular beauty of themself is enough. And hopefully that day comes soon.

You're going to feel like you have to be validated by cis society to truly be a woman. You'll think that if they don't approve, you might as well not have transitioned at all. That is 100% not true. Your gender and presentation only needs the validation of yourself.
Cassiopeia Violet Drake

DISCOMFORT WITH TERMINOLOGY

While there is no single transgender experience, many trans people feel a deep, disturbing disconnect between their gender and their physical beings. External sex characteristics like genitalia and breasts can be dysphoria triggers, which means the terminology associated with those body parts can also be painful. The words you used previously to refer to your beloved's anatomy may no longer be appropriate, even the nicknames, affectionate descriptors, and inside jokes.

The loss of established ways of communicating with your beloved about their body may be painful, but it can be an avenue for deepening intimacy as you develop new ways of referring to body parts together.

Some trans individuals appreciate having their chest referred to using the terminology associated with their gender: for example, calling a transmasculine person's chest "pecs." For other people, this approach can be dysphoria triggering, and so developing new terms works better.

If you're having trouble coming up with terminology, consider reaching out to support groups to ask what's worked for other couples in your situation. They may have suggestions.

Handle them carefully, for words have more power than atom bombs.
Pearl Strachan Hurd

ROUTINE ACTIVITIES MIGHT GET HARDER

Trans people spend lifetimes equipping themselves to live as the gender they were assigned at birth. The physical realities and social demands of being a particular sex require routines that are part of maintaining that false persona. Trans women shave their faces and cut their hair short. Trans men cope with menstruation and shave legs and armpits. It's simply the way things are.

But once a person begins to taste the freedom of gender authenticity, these activities can transform from daily drudgery to something much more painful. Even showering can be an excruciating reminder their body is not aligned with their essential being.

Changing the way these activities are performed can assuage the discomfort a bit. For example, some trans people shower in a bathing suit. Razor types can be swapped for those marketed toward your beloved's gender. The use of period underwear (particularly in boxer-brief shapes) can reduce the dysphoria of having to carry and change sanitary napkins or tampons. These products can be ordered online or shopped for by you to further reduce the triggers.

Many of our gender presentation demands are silly, and hopefully one of the benefits of your partner's transition will be to help you both recognize the inanity of these cultural expectations. The more publicly a person is out, the more they can release culturally demanded gender routines. But the transition away from these expectations can be hard for your loved one, and it's best to be prepared for that pain.

My experience of being trans is a complete loss of sexuality, loss of privilege, loss of friends and sometimes family, loss of—well pretty much everything—only to gain the simple ability to honestly exist in this world as the person you've known you were all along.
Amy Hicox

GUILT

In the previous section we talked about the feelings of guilt *you* experience. Today we talk about those your loved one grapples with.

Transgender men may feel heartsick at the thought of their children becoming motherless. Females are enculturated to be self-denying and caregiving, and self-sacrifice is seen as a virtue. Recognizing the need for authenticity can feel selfish, even when it's emotional survival. Since trans men were formed within this system, they have to work through the process of rejecting it's hold.

Transgender women may worry about the impact coming out will have on their children in the same ways, or in different ones. The toxic masculinity pervading so much of western culture demands that men maintain personas of strength, stoicism, and capability, and so transfeminine people may worry about male children not having a role model to help conform them to those norms.

All trans folx can feel guilty about the perceived losses their parents and spouses experience, and the life changes that come along with transitioning. They can regret ways they handled various issues in the distant past or more recently. Guilt can be particularly insidious for those raised in dysfunctional settings resulting in codependency.

The causes of guilt feelings are many, but here are some strategies your partner can employ to help cope with them:

- Acknowledge the pain others experience without apologizing for the reality of their gender identity.

- Recognize the importance of self-focus. It won't last forever.

- Seek the opinions of those who can be objective when guilt feelings make it difficult to see clearly.

- Practice self-forgiveness.

Your beloved may not have handled everything perfectly in the past, but we humans rarely do. The stressors on transgender people are intense, and it's impossible not to occasionally crack. Managing feelings of guilt in a healthy way is an important step forward in the transition journey.

Shame is the lie someone told you about yourself.
Anais Nin

HORMONE THERAPIES AND SURGERY

Transgender people are transgender whether they take medical action to shift their gender presentation or whether they take no action whatsoever. Some trans individuals desire high degrees of medical intervention to align their bodies more closely with their gender identity. Others don't want any. There is no right or wrong way to be trans.

Researching gender-affirmation therapies and procedures is crucial, because decisions related to them are intensely personal and vary based on health conditions, degree of and triggers for dysphoria, financial considerations, and other issues.

There are many reliable sources of medical information available online and we're not going to talk about the details in this space. But here are just a few short points for you to be aware of as you begin investigating:

- Hormones aren't magic. They won't do everything your beloved wishes they could do. Some people experience swift, dramatic shifts, others find the changes subtler and slower to come. Results vary significantly, and realizing this can help your partner minimize disappointment. Celebrating even small shifts is helpful.

- Some transgender care providers require a structured process of evaluation and counseling before hormone therapies are started. This means that when working through them, it can take quite a while to begin. Surgery takes even longer. "Informed consent" clinics use a streamlined approach, and you can do an online search to find the ones closest to you.

- Cisgender people can be unintentionally obtuse about how to discuss the transition process. You and your partner may be faced with rude questions related to the types of medical interventions you plan to implement, if any. Planning appropriate responses to inappropriate questions ahead of time is useful.

- Transgender health care is a growing field of interest, but the relative newness means there's a good chance your beloved and you may know more about options and issues than the providers you initially visit.

Decision making about medical treatments is complex. Arming yourself with information helps you arrive at the best possible plan for moving forward.

I think it's really difficult for folks that aren't transgender to really wrap their mind around the feeling of having a gender identity that differs from their sex assigned at birth. But for me, it felt like a constant feeling of homesickness.
Sarah McBride

THEY MAY WANT TO MOVE QUICKLY

People who've spent a lifetime in hiding may be impatient to stop. They may feel like they've reached the point where they simply can't do it anymore, and their spirit screams for freedom and authenticity. It grates on the soul to lie. Maintaining a constant pretense goes against the hunger for truth woven into our spiritual DNA.

For some relationships moving quickly is manageable. Both parties are able to shift, families and social circles are open and accepting, and jobs are not at risk. For other couples, transition can be wrenching and disruptive of all those things.

If you're in the situation where your partner is desperate to move forward with transitioning but the structure of your life makes it complicated, you're in a pretty tough spot. You'll need to negotiate the timing together.

Try to come up with a set of rules for how various decisions for timing will be made. For example, you could decide that each of you chooses how and when to tell members of your respective families, but that you'll determine the timing for mutual friends together. Financial considerations are also something you might decide should be determined jointly.

Timing is sensitive, tricky, and unique to individual situations. Reassure your beloved that you support their desire to be open and honest about who they are to the degree that they feel comfortable. The assurance that you're with them as you figure out details for communication relieves some of the pressure of the waiting.

I have a boy's body, and that body happens to have a vagina.
Whether the world knows it or not, this is a boy's body. My body
belongs to me.
Declan DeWitt Hall

EXPECT EXPERIMENTATION

From the moment we're born, we have influential people in our life who teach us how to be the gender we're assigned. These lessons are both spoken and unspoken, through direct teaching or by role-modeling. Trans people must unlearn those teachings and retrain into the person they want to be.

Here's how transgender researcher Dr. Ruth Pearce describes it:

> *At the time of writing, I am 10 years old, 14 years old, and 30 years old. I was born 30 years ago; in chronological terms, I have lived for 30 years. Chronological time is, however, just one means by which ageing might be understood. When we talk about age in terms of chronological time, we make a number of assumptions. Most importantly, we assume that our journey through the life course is linear, progressing from birth (at the beginning of the journey) to death (at the end). But my age can also be understood in terms of trans time. As a trans woman, I have experienced non-linear temporalities of disruption, disjuncture, and discontinuity.[5]*

People who transition as adults didn't have the chance to do things that ordinarily take place over the course of years, for example, developing a personal style. They didn't get to try on glittery heels for prom or experiment with goatees and soul patches. Our parents were occasionally frustrated or embarrassed when we experimented with too much eyeliner and short skirts, or expensive sneakers and angry-slogan-embellished tee shirts. But they loved us through it. That's your job now.

Expect experimentation. Your beloved may choose a name and discover it doesn't fit. They may test their emotions to figure out if it's okay for a transmasculine person to cry. They might experiment with behaviors to convey toughness or fragility.

---

[5] *Trans Temporalities and Non-Linear Ageing,* www.ruthpearce.net, 2018.

Like our parents, we have to be careful with our suggestions, and patient with the process. We all deserve to look, dress, and act the way we want, as long as it's not intended to harm others.

You can find ways to help your loved one re-experience significant milestones, and the process can be fun! Have dance parties with music from decades past. Recreate a prom. Get some clothes from the era to wear at home. Have a series of birthday parties for age 5, 10, 15, and 20. Find out what toy or item they wanted at particular ages and get it for them. Relive having a drink for the first time when they came of age. Experiencing these kinds of things may help your loved one move through the awkward adolescent phases more quickly and smoothly.

It's helpful to have a conversation early in the process about the kind of input your partner would like about style choices. This can be a fruitful time to discuss societal perceptions, your own views on the intentionality of gender presentation (or lack of it), and perhaps even do your own experimentation.

There is great opportunity in this season of exploration. Your beloved gets to weigh different modes of expressing masculinity and femininity, adopting traits and behaviors that are useful and healthy, and discarding those that are damaging to self or others. And you can do the same.

Self-definition and self-determination are about the many varied decisions that we make to compose and journey toward ourselves... It's OK if your personal definition is in a constant state of flux as you navigate the world.
Janet Mock

THEY MAY WANT TO MOVE SLOWLY

Transitioning is a process of moving into something new. But that means it's also movement *out* of a lifetime of collected experiences, behaviors, and coping mechanisms. Your loved one spent years developing systems for choosing the least bad of a set of bad options regarding everything from sock styles to behaviors.

Humans take comfort in routines, even the irritating ones, and loss of them can be destabilizing. Because of this, for some couples, the transitioning person might have more fears than their partner does. You might feel ready for things to move along, while your beloved struggles through all sorts of decisions, large and small. They face a tornado of concerns and emotions. Worries about safety, family impact, dysphoria, timing and health risks for treatments and procedures, and sometimes trumping all the rest: whether or not they'll eventually be able to "pass."

Trans people spent decades managing life in the gender assigned at birth. Even if you've been together for a long time, you'll never have as much emotional or intellectual investment in the framework of lifelong unwanted pretense.

Because of this, the timing of transition must be up to the person transitioning. Both of you are in a process of deconstructing life as you've known it. It takes time to do that. But while various decisions can and should be made together, when it comes to how fast or slow to go, the pace needs to be set by them.

To come out as a trans woman in a transphobic patriarchal society that views our existence as a curiosity at best is rarely something done all at once. It requires baby steps, like becoming used to a new name that starts to feel like home.
Emily VanDerWerff

76

BATHROOMS ARE A BIG DEAL

Bathrooms often aren't safe. Transmasculine people are at risk of being beaten up or raped. Transfeminine people are at risk of being accused of nefarious intentions and being assaulted by the "defenders" of other females once they exit the facilities.

Safety isn't the only challenge. As transgender people increasingly embrace their true gender the discomfort of using restrooms aligning with their sex assigned at birth similarly increases. Even if they haven't shifted their gender presentation significantly, simply knowing they're in an intimate space with people of the opposite sex who think they're one of them feels uncomfortable.

In the early days of transition it may not seem like it should be a big deal for your partner to use the restroom they've always used. But it *is* a big deal, and you can help. Non-gendered facilities and family restrooms are becoming more common and give transgender people options. In our town there are two home improvement stores. One has a family restroom, the other does not. We frequent the one that does. This might be true for the grocery and big box stores in your area, and you can take your commerce there. If you're planning a night out including dinner, call around to find places that make bathroom spaces accessible and trans-friendly. If you're going on a road trip, identify gas station and restaurant chains where non-gendered restrooms are the norm.

The simple human need to use a restroom shouldn't be so complicated, but it is. Bathrooms are a big deal.

The funny thing is that the fear hurts you. It's the not knowing if something else is going to come up the next time you go to the bathroom, it's the vigilance that affected me and my well-being more than anything, more than the attacks that never materialized. It was the anticipation of the possible attack. And I still live with that when I go into men's rooms.
Mitch Kellaway

THEY MAY WORRY THEY AREN'T ENOUGH

As your loved one transitions, they may go through phases of questioning their value. They might feel repulsive to you emotionally or physically, or worry about being man or woman enough (whatever that means) to meet your needs. The more thoughtful and loving your partner is, the more this issue might impact them.

But the opposite is actually true: trans people are more.

In cultures all over the world, people who cross the gender binary in various ways have deep respect within their communities. For many cultures, those individuals act as mediators between the spiritual world and the physical, because their beings more closely reflect the dual male/female nature of the divine. And it's not about how publicly that gender presentation is conveyed, it's about the specialness of their very being.

They might also feel like they aren't trans enough compared to someone else's public transformation. We humans have a hard time not trying to keep up with the Joneses.

If your beloved feels like they aren't enough, your default response might be to simply assure them that where they are is fine. But it's not your journey, and satisfaction with their transition can only be experienced by them. Instead, remind them that their current stage is valuable—for right now and for the days to come—and that their inherent worth shines through all the external manifestations of identity.

Trans people aren't less than cisgender people, they're simply different, and that difference brings a unique beauty to the world.

Do not wish to be anything but what you are, and try to be that perfectly.
Francis de Sales

THEY MAY DECIDE TO STOP

For some people, the emotional cost of transitioning is too high. The older a person is, the harder it can be to transition. Many people turn away from the potential for freedom out of fear they'll experience even more pain if they detransition later. Fear of loss can win out over hope of gain.

It's important to understand that no one can return to the persona they were prior to coming out. Once they've stepped through the door something significant and integral shifts within them. If fear or relational disruption causes them to go back into hiding, they won't be who or what they were before. They can't be. They will be different because they *are* different.

And so are you.

Like transitioning, detransitioning is a process: a step-by-step deaccumulation of gender-related milestones, many of which are interior. It's not like flipping a switch, even if a person hasn't had hormone therapy or gender affirmation surgery. The longer they've been transitioning, the longer it takes to move backward.

Reversing transition carries an emotional toll, but it's not up to you to decide for your beloved. Hopefully the two of you are intimate enough to have the kinds of discussions that help reach the right answers for them. You shouldn't pressure them into stopping, hurriedly agree with stopping, or hamper their stopping. This is a situation in which you need to give them space and freedom to work through their decision. If you demand your beloved's transition ceases, your relationship will pay the price and the cost can be higher than you've imagined.

All people should have the right to live as themselves. But doing so sometimes feels like too much, and detransition happens. It's their gender, it's their journey, it's their life. All you can do is be a sounding board as they work through it.

It's perhaps the root of the Christian abuse, the teaching that your body is not yours. It's God's. It's your husbands. It's made for specific reasons that are determined by church. You do not know or own your body. Body is what makes us. Body has always been their biggest enemy.
Elle Finke

GRIEVING THE LOSSES

YOUR BELOVED IS NOT DEAD

With a change as significant as transition, losses are pretty much guaranteed to be a byproduct. You might feel like your world is falling apart, and that everything about life as you know it is shifting. In this section, we'll talk about various kinds of grief you might experience, because acknowledging and dealing with loss is important.

The most obvious and immediate sensation could be feeling as if your partner has died. This is a heartrending and common emotion, even though they're still physically with you. You may need to experience this sensation in order for it to pass, but try not to say it to your beloved. When you do, it makes them feel like you loved who they were forced to pretend to be rather than who they really are.

To help move through this phase of grief, try thinking back to what drew you together in the first place. What personality traits were attractive? Was it their sense of humor, their intelligence, their compassion? Those essential character traits are core pieces of their beings, regardless of how they present gender.

Here's how one person described their emotional arc as they processed these feelings:

It feels like looking at pics of my kids when they were babies. I miss that child at that stage, and I also love who they've grown to be now. I wouldn't change that growth, but I still miss my child at that stage and long for that at times. It's something akin to grief but not quite grief—it's very bittersweet. It comes and goes in waves.

84

It's okay to feel sad that the memories you make in the future won't match those from the past, and to miss aspects of the way things were. It's okay to mourn. But try not to make your loved one feel like they've died. They're still here.

When you hear the same stories over and over again, from people from all over the world, you start realizing that transgender is not an anomaly. It's a part of the spectrum of people's realities. Then you stop wondering about the cause and you start realizing it's a part of reality.

Susan Kuklin

THE PROCESS OF GRIEF

If we don't permit ourselves to mourn, our emotion sublimates and can reappear in destructive ways, impacting our health, our relationships, our trust, and our peace. We'll talk about various kinds of loss in the coming days. Today we discuss the importance of grief itself.

Grief frequently manifests in the phases and stages described below.

Denial: When your beloved shares their truth with you and you begin to contemplate various kinds of loss, an early reaction is denial. Our minds sometimes cope with an overload of emotion by simply pretending that reality isn't what it is.

Anger: You might find yourself angry that life used to be simpler, or feel misled. You might be angry at yourself for not recognizing the truth, or for having such a hard time accepting it. You can even be angry at God.

Bargaining: As you grapple with loss you might try to make deals with your loved one, yourself, or the divine.

Guilt: We discussed guilt feelings in detail in the previous sections. As part of the grieving process, you might feel guilt about the grief itself, about actions and behaviors from the past, or about not knowing if we can hold up under the strain of what's happening in your lives.

Depression: Feeling depressed is common when relationships encounter shifts as significant as transition.

Acceptance: The process of mourning is important and necessary, and out of it eventually comes acceptance, which brings a measure of peace.

Reconstruction: As acceptance settles in, new ways of viewing life begin to surface.

Your own grief process might unfold in the order listed, in other orders, or in overlapping waves and circles. Hopefully your partner has compassion for the losses you'll experience. If they struggle to demonstrate understanding, consider discussing it in a counseling or other mediated setting, where a third party can help break down barriers to communication.

Mourning is important. Give yourself the painful gift of experiencing it, so you can shake through to a new era of growth and opportunity.

Grief isn't linear. It's not a 5-step process where you find a solution or a fix. Grief stays with us. I learned from experience; if we do the work of naming and processing grief, it can evolve, and we can learn to befriend and live with grief. It's OK to grieve.

James Prescott

LOSS OF PERCEIVED STABILITY

When your partner comes out to you, it can feel like the ground beneath you is buckling and you have no idea when it will stop or what the world will be like once it does. The stability you envisioned as bedrock to your relationship seems to have fractured.

But here's a hard reality: it was merely a perceived stability, and a potentially false one. Your beloved was trans before they came out, even if you didn't recognize it.

You aren't alone in this experience. Both of you will face fears about whether your relationship can weather the shift. They may be afraid you won't be able to accept and love them. You may be afraid they'll want to live a new and different life, a life you won't be part of. And it's possible these things are true.

Both of you may mourn the loss of the time before, when things seemed simpler and more stable. But the loss is really of a perception, and of a false state of being. When a person is living a lie, security is a hard feeling to achieve. The lack of transparency causes foundational cracks in relationships. Misrepresentations are corrosive to both the one who conveys them, and the one who receives them.

The loss of perceived stability is a real thing. Even recognizing that it was a false reality creates loss.

Grieve these things. Feel the pain. Admit it exists. Only then can you move on to create a new kind of security, this time, based on truth.

Until our certitudes and our own little self-written success stories begin to fall apart, we usually won't touch upon any form of deeper wisdom.
Richard Rohr

LOSS OF A PARTICULAR IMAGE OF FAMILY

People grow up under many different models of family. We might be raised by single moms, grandparents, a cisgender mom and dad, or gay parents. Emotionally healthy relationships or dysfunction can be formed within each model. No matter what your family of origin was like, you've undoubtedly created an image for what an optimal family unit means, and have hopes and dreams about creating it.

You may have pictured the stereotypical mom and dad with 2.5 kids, and suddenly you're facing a quite different structure. Or you may have dreamt of being wonderful lesbian parents to a single, perfect child, or the best possible dads to a pair of adopted siblings. When your loved one comes out as trans, all these dreams need to shift. You'll be faced with the loss of that particular view of the future.

If you expected your FTM spouse would get pregnant, this assumption may have to be revisited because carrying a baby for a trans man can be excruciating. And MTF individuals may desire therapies that impact fertility. Some couples choose to freeze eggs or sperm for later use, though costs can be prohibitive.

Looking at wedding albums, old family photos, and other items saturated with meaning related to the idea of family can trigger that sense of loss for both you and your beloved. While the future is rarely how we envision it and your dreams would probably have shifted for reasons other than this, the loss of your idea of family is real. Honoring it will help you move forward.

I was not ladylike, nor was I manly. I was something else altogether.
There were so many different ways to be beautiful.
Michael Cunningham

LOSS OF ROLES AND IDENTITY

It's natural for people to fall into roles within family structures. When your partner decides to transition, it might feel as if your accustomed roles are threatened. If you've been the only dad, son, or brother in the family all these years, certain understandings and behaviors were expected for that role. When a transmasculine family member comes out, it can shift this dynamic so you're no longer the only guy. The same goes for females and their roles.

This can be particularly true for parental roles in families where western understandings of traditional gender performance are followed. For example, in stereotypically "traditional" family structures, a mother may consider her value as being closely tied to the things she does to take care of the children and the household. If the person she thought of as husband transitions, how much might they want to step into the motherly role? Fathers in these circumstances face the same kinds of fear and loss when a spouse desires to take on activities which have been their responsibility until now.

If you're gay or lesbian, the shift can also make you question what your sexual orientation is now. One spouse of a trans person said this:

> I worked hard for the victory to marry as a gay person, and to come out to those who judged me. Am I straight now?

This is a valid question, and one which can only be answered through contemplation and conversation. There is no one way to be trans, and no one way to be the partner of a trans person.

It's common for partners of transgender people to question their identity when their loved one comes out. All of this is an opportunity for growth in understanding our value, separate from the roles we play, responsibilities we hold, and actions we perform.

Life is just a constant invitation to find out how vast you are.
Jeff Foster

LOSS OF A SEX OBJECT

You might worry that you can't be sexually attracted to the person your significant other has had to hide all these years. Maybe physical attraction played a key role in how the two of you originally connected. Perhaps it's still an integral element to your sexual intimacy. But even when that's the case, there are also deeper levels than the shape and hairiness of their body, the pitch of their voice, and the kind of pants they wear.

Or at least, I hope there are.

In good relationships, sex offers a unique kind of union between beloveds. Sure there is pleasure, but there's also a special bonding, a draw and union of two spirits, and a connection that goes far deeper than skin level.

If you're having trouble envisioning your loved one as the object of your sexual attraction given their shifting gender expression, try to remember the depth experienced in your best physical encounters; times when you felt especially connected, heart to heart, soul to soul. That kind of connection is still possible if you both want to achieve it.

To explore the potential for deepening intimacy and connection, check out *Sex With God: Meditations on the sacred nature of sex in a post-purity-culture world*. It was written with the goal of doing just that.

People aren't objects; they're tender, strong, vulnerable souls. Sexuality is a spectrum, and we're all our own little dot of moisture in the mist that makes up a rainbow. Having a partner transition can result in a deepened intimacy, where objectification is removed.

If only our eyes saw souls instead of bodies how different our ideals of
beauty would be.
Lauren Jauregui

92

LOSS OF COMMUNITY

Each of us belongs to a variety of overlapping communities. We have the people we work with, our friends, those at the schools we or our children attend, parenting groups, religious organizations, volunteer associations, hobbyist groups, and others. Each community is composed of individuals with wide-ranging views on LGBTQIA+ issues. When your loved one goes public about their gender identity, there will be ripples in all these collections of people. Reactions are sometimes severe enough that you'll decide you no longer want to participate in them.

Making these decisions results in real loss. The monthly book club or weekly night out with friends might have played a significant role in your social roster and your emotional health. When faith is important to you, the loss of regular participation in activities of church or other religious organizations is particularly painful.

If behavior within any group violates laws or governing principles, they should be reported through appropriate channels. Taking action helps vent anger and pain.

Over time you'll find new, affirming communities to replace those lost, and the new ones will be better able to embrace the diverse mix of humanity of which the world is composed. That's a good thing. But the shift will hurt, and your heart, mind, and body may all need time to grieve.

I've never really understood why so many Christians feel the need to use the Bible to try and figure everything out. "Love God and love your neighbors as you love yourself" is a work that, quite frankly, lasts a lifetime. There will always be new depths of love to plunge into.
Jimmy Tidmore

LOSS OF SPECIFIC THINGS

The losses we've discussed so far have been pretty big things, but some of the stuff you'll need to grieve is in the fine details. You might mourn that the voice of your beloved is changing. You might be sad that a particular part of your loved one's body is being reduced, removed, or simply changed. You might miss saying the name you've always known them by. Then there's the sensory items: the feel of a furry chest, the smell of a particular perfume. One partner said their beloved's scent smelled like home and were sad about missing that experience.

You'll lose terminology for concepts like mom, dad, sister, brother, wife, and husband. You might miss being the only girl or guy in the house. Gay and lesbian couples can be sad about not going into restrooms together. Some things just won't ever be the same, and life may never be as simple as it was.

It's not fair to deprive anyone of living in freedom and integrity just so we don't have to deal with a period of temporary discomfort. You'll adjust to the shifts in the small, specific things as long as your relationship can survive the big shifts. But it's perfectly okay to mourn them.

Transition is a fire, clearing the way for the most durable tree in the forest to bloom and grow without limit. The part of you that remains is the part of you that cannot be destroyed. That soul in you that always was, and always will be. The now burnt forest in you, is what any passing tourist would have said that you were before, because in those moments, to them, you actually were. When they paused in awe your majestic oaks, the flocks of birds in your branches, the moss and the dandelions and the flowers, you heard them and you believed them. Though you knew it wasn't the best part of you—the most durable part—it was beautiful. And you wanted that for yourself. So, now that it's all gone to ash. There is the now present, and forever longed for beauty of unfettered life. And there is grief for the lost illusions. And there is the constant learning and relearning. "I wasn't the forest; I was the strongest tree in it."
Amy Hicox

CREATE A RITE OF MOURNING

The previous reflections in this section focused on losses you might encounter after your partner comes out as transgender. Trans people also mourn all sorts of things. They grieve the lost years, the limits to the physical changes they can make to align with their gender identity, the people who reject or condemn them, and so much more. Today we discuss the power of formally acknowledging that grief.

Memorial services are important milestones in the grieving process, which help those in mourning move forward in adjusting to the new normal. Creating a rite of mourning can help you both. I've provided a sample format in Appendix B that you can use as a starting point. If you're person of faith, you can ask a clergy person to help tailor it or create your own.

Remember that this isn't a funeral for the person you thought your partner was. Treating their transition as a death is powerfully damaging. But you can mourn the fact that you were under a false impression and that things will not be the way you envisioned. They can mourn the things they didn't get to experience throughout their childhood, teen years, and adulthood so far. And if your marriage can't survive the shifts underway, the ceremony can even honor that.

Humans are creatures for whom ritual and liturgy are valuable tools. Make use of that facility to help further your emotional health and healing.

This is what rituals are for. We do spiritual ceremonies as human beings in order to create a safe resting place for our most complicated feelings of joy or trauma, so that we don't have to haul those feelings around with us forever, weighing us down. We all need such places of ritual safekeeping.
Elizabeth Gilbert

TANGIBLE HELPFULNESS

BUILD A SUPPORT CIRCLE

We all need support, even during mundane phases of life, and the need escalates at times of significant shifts and stress.

It's extremely helpful for trans people to share challenges and victories with those who understand what it's like. There's freedom in being able to simply be themselves within that space, without feeling judged. Support groups are also a source of knowledge about how to make transition and trans life easier.

It's just as important for *you* to have a support cohort who understands what you're going through. You need safe places to vent, ask questions, learn, and cry. You'll need circles of encouragement for you, for your partner, and for the two of you as a unit; a Venn diagram of supporters for when either of you feel hurt by each other or by those in the world who don't understand.

At times it might feel like your loved one connects more with their support community than they do with you, and in some cases this can be true. They may feel safer talking with others who understand their reality intimately. They may be worried about your outward reactions and your inward emotions. They might want to shield you from pain. It's also possible that they aren't intentionally excluding you, but your emotions are so ragged that it just feels that way. Your interactions with your support system may make them feel similarly excluded. Even so, the support is needed.

Transitioning is emotional. Being intentional about recognizing this reality helps manage the emotion for both of you.

The world can visit its hate and violence on you, and it's awful, and it should change, and there's no excuse for what this country wants to put vulnerable people through. But the power of your community is something that cannot be taken by force. And then it's no longer oppression vs. isolated individuals. You're not alone. And even when you are alone, you're not. You're part of something ancient, and powerful: the sum of thousands of miracles. Suddenly justice doesn't seem so unlikely. "We" can do what "I" can't.
Lyra Foster

EXAMINE FAITH ISSUES FROM A DIFFERENT LENS

People of faith face particular challenges when considering transition. Followers of Abrahamic religions like Judaism, Islam, and Christianity may have been taught that being transgender is offensive to God. If this is the case for you or your loved one, you're being invited to take a closer look at things you've never had to analyze before. This examination can be scary, but can also lead to a richer understanding of the structures of faith, and a deeper connection to the divine.

For many cultures around the globe, non-binary people are viewed as being better able to connect to the spiritual world, because divinity is commonly viewed as either having no gender or being both male and female. People who do not fall into the binary male versus female model are therefore seen as more fully reflective of the divine nature. Within Abrahamic faith traditions however there are varying degrees of disapproval, disparagement, or worse depending on the scriptural and dogmatic teaching passed down through individual sects, denominations, and congregations.

If you're struggling with this, there are resources to help you evaluate what your understanding of God is, what the role of scripture should play in that understanding, and whether or not the divine is calling you to re-form some of the views you absorbed through your faith formation. If you're Christian, you can check out my *Where True Love Is, I don't Want Them to Go to Hell,* and *Transfigured* devotionals, which deal with these issues. There are similar resources for other faith traditions.

The creative power of love that formed us in their image and likeness appreciates our seeking to know them better. As you enter into examining God's view of gender more intensively, pray that your mind and heart will be open to the Spirit's whisper, and closed to everything else.

People of deep and abiding faith have widely varying views about gender identity and concepts of righteousness. This may be a time for you to examine these issues from a different lens, and see what God wants to show you.

In order to have important conversations, you will sometimes have to check your opinions at the door. There is no belief so strong that it cannot be set aside temporarily in order to learn from someone who disagrees. Don't worry; your beliefs will still be there when you're done.
Celeste Headlee

EXPECT HOLIDAYS TO BE HARD

Emotions run high at holidays, and special days on the calendar add emotional complexity to the transgender experience, particularly in the first year of coming out.

Mother's Day and Father's Day are hard for trans parents as both they and the children work out how to view their roles and titles.

Birthdays can trigger sorrow in trans people for the years they were forced to hide, or despair that they aren't young enough to take transition steps they would consider if they were younger. They might be sad they can't live as openly as they want to, and feel like the coming years in the closet will be long.

When family members have struggled to accept your loved one's transition, long-standing holiday traditions and rituals may be uncomfortable, or you may choose not to engage at all due to the disruption they could cause.

Experiencing these emotions is natural, so it's wise to plan for managing events like this. If you have to opt out of traditional holiday or celebration activities, plan something entirely new to replace them. If you normally cook a particular menu and spend the day at home, consider going on an adventure together instead, or eat at an unusual restaurant, or pack a picnic and go somewhere to breathe fresh air. Hold a dance party for two in your living room. Take a donation or treats to a transgender support organization in your area, or to fire departments, emergency rooms, or other places where people have to work while others have the day off.

Finding new ways to celebrate helps eases the pain of not being able to honor holidays in the ways you're used to. It doesn't fix it entirely, but it helps.

Trying to take up as little space as possible only pleases people who don't want you there in the first place.
Merryn Armstrong

IDENTIFY GOALS AND MILESTONES

Trans people have a lot of decisions to make about things they want to accomplish and the pace for moving forward. It can be very hard to figure out what to do, and they can get stuck on the idea that they'll never win the race. But what *is* the race? What does the finish line look like? At what point will your loved one feel like they're male, female, or trans *enough*?

Each trans person must decide what their own goals are, because there's no measuring stick for what constitutes "real" masculinity or femininity. There are no scientific tests to confirm a person's gender, and no way of being the right kind of trans. Helping your loved one realize this can ground their thinking so they can better evaluate what their ultimate goals are, and then break those goals into actionable steps to take them along that path.

Here's an example of a goals list:

- Presenting gender authentically at home.
- Having a wardrobe for use at home.
- Being out to family.
- Being out to friends.
- Having a wardrobe of work clothing.
- Being out at work.
- Presenting gender authentically at work.
- Not having to fake it at family gatherings.
- Understanding hormone replacement therapy options.
- Understanding gender confirmation surgery options.

Creating a timeline for achieving various goals can help manage your loved one's frustration and your own anxiety about what's to come.

Once you've captured goals, break each one into milestones and the actions it takes to achieve them. For example, milestones might be that all your children have been told, that all undergarments have been replaced, and that a hormone therapy consultation has taken place. Tasks within those milestones would be to talk to a particular child, to purchase tee shirts, and to schedule the appointment.

Approaching issues in a structured way may not be your default mode of operation, but if the two of you can agree to give it a try, you could find that the process relieves pressure and helps you focus on what can be done rather than what's impossible.

Most trans women won't eventually have the curves of a Barbie doll (few cisgender women do). Most trans men won't eventually have a voice with the depth and resonance of Barry White (few cisgender men do). Some things may simply never be achievable, and those things may need to be mourned. But in all circumstances, actions of authenticity *can* be taken. Identifying achievable states offers hope, which your partner desperately needs and deserves.

> *If you want to be happy, set a goal that commands your thoughts,*
> *liberates your energy, and inspires your hopes.*
> Andrew Carnegie

CELEBRATE ACHIEVEMENTS

The transition process is an ongoing journey rather than a destination, with moments of both elation and fear. Sometimes the process will feel like two steps forward and five back. This goes for both you and your partner. You'll both need encouragement.

Because of this, it's important to savor and celebrate things that go well. Small moments of euphoria are big moments to hold on to. Once you've made your list of goals and milestones, celebrate as each one is achieved. Heck, even celebrate that you created the list!

It generally works best to think about ways to celebrate ahead of time. You could get a special candle to light after small victories are achieved, or purchase encouragement cards to cheer them on. The two of you can plan together how to celebrate bigger milestones. For example, you might go to a special place with a picnic and a bottle of something bubbly to toast as the sun goes down. When name changes are finalized, you could burn bills or other documents bearing their dead name to commemorate the end of that phase of life.

Celebrate when people accept their coming out with grace and acceptance. Celebrate when a new piece of clothing works. Celebrate when a medical appointment goes well. Keep track of these victories, big and small, and revisit the list when things aren't quite so rosy.

Transitioning is an emotional process. Celebrating achievements helps keep spirits up and maintain balance.

Gender transition requires a non-standard relationship to winning.
It has to be about small, incremental goals, not a sudden becoming.
The slow pace and difficulty of it doesn't mean you're losing. It just
means you need to rethink what winning means.
Kiri Anne Ryan Stewart

DEVELOP PLANS

Earlier we talked about the usefulness of breaking goals down into milestones and tasks. Today we continue the idea of planning, but this time for the purpose of preventing problems.

You and your beloved face a host of unknowns about the future and about individual situations comprising ordinary life. One way of managing worry and reducing problematic scenarios is to develop plans for issues that have higher chances for uncertainty or difficulty.

Here are some kinds of plans to consider:

- What to do if you can't find appropriate bathrooms.

- How to handle changing rooms. (A few suggestions: order clothes online, find out what stores have the simplest return policies so your partner can try them on at home, and identify stores that don't have gendered changing rooms.)

- How to respond if you encounter confrontational people.

- How to control your anger so that problematic situations don't escalate.

- What to do if safety is threatened. (Consider purchasing pepper spray and alarms or whistles, studying self-defense techniques, identifying places likely to offer sanctuary, etc.)

Role playing to practice handling these situations can be helpful.

The more scenarios you identify for potential embarrassment, inconvenience, or danger, the better equipped you'll both be for dealing with whatever life throws your way.

We've all known the long loneliness and we've learned that the only solution is love and that love comes with community.
Dorothy Day

MANAGING SHIFTS IN SEXUAL INTERACTION

Sexuality is an intensely important part of the human condition and varies from person to person and couple to couple. For most people, gender plays a significant role in how we engage sexually, and so transition impacts this key aspect of our lives.

Trans people may struggle with dissociative experiences during sex prior to coming out.[6] Deep intimacy can be hard to achieve, since they can't connect with the other person as their authentic selves. Escaping from these patterns once they're free to express their gender can take time.

Shifts in your beloved's gender presentation could impact your experience of physical intimacy with them. Being raised within purity culture introduces special challenges, for example, you may question whether it's okay to be in a sexual relationship with someone of the same gender. Sexual trauma further complicates things. If you've experienced abuse or assault, you may have a hard time acclimating to sexual intimacy if your partner is the gender of the perpetrator.

Depending on emotional state, hormonal interventions, and other shifts, your partner's interest in sex may decline, their sex drive might increase, and/or their way of initiating and communicating about sex may change. A transitioning person may question their role as initiator versus recipient of advances and feel unsure about how they're "supposed" to act.

All of these things can create relationship disruption. We tend to feel vulnerable about our bodies and sexuality, so discussions about these issues require intentionally sensitive handling. Some couples find that not thinking of penetrative sex as the main event can be helpful, instead, considering all the ways of giving and receiving physical pleasure as full parts of satisfying sexual

---

[6] *Depersonalization in gender dysphoria: widespread and widely unrecognized,* www.genderanalysis.net, 2017.

engagement. Genital-to-genital contact is wonderful, but your entire body has the potential to be a sex organ.

Sexual excitement and attraction to a spouse or long-term partner waxes and wanes over time in all relationships. Lulls can occur during emotional states like mourning or stress. Sex drive can lessen when you're so busy that you're exhausted, which is common during the early years of parenting. Sexual interaction can also decrease as the years pass and our bodies age, becoming more intensely centered around the unity, comfort, and pleasure you create together rather than the steaminess of earlier romance. Variation in sexual desire is nearly universal. For a couple that includes a transgender partner, the shifts simply come from additional causes.

Not all relationships can survive the storms. But moving through this together can lead to unexpected healing of sexual brokenness, simply through the act of facing issues that have not been dealt with.

We should all seek to connect not merely our bodies through sex, but also our hearts, minds, and spirits. If the two of you can push through the challenges of shifting sexual desires, you can reach new levels of intimacy through lovemaking.[7]

It is not always easy to be joyful, to keep in mind the duty of delight.
Dorothy Day

---

[7] Check out my *Sex With God* devotional for a deeper exploration of the interconnection of sexuality and spirituality.

CREATE AND SUPPORT RITES OF PASSAGE

Bar mitzvahs, quinceañeras, getting a driver's permit, and graduating from school are major milestones and celebrations of significant shifts in a person's life. Transgender individuals often miss out on the rituals corresponding with their identity, even things as prosaic as the first time menstruating or learning how to shave. Some of these milestones simply can't be replicated, but others can, and new experiences can be created to help mark the process of transitioning.

Rites of passage could include:

- Going through closets and dressers to get rid of clothing that doesn't reflect your loved one's reality.

- Shopping for new clothes. Undergarments can have particular poignance and significance.

- Replacing jewelry.

- Purchasing razors marketed toward your loved one's gender.

- Having makeup applied by someone who's really good at it.

- Practicing signing their chosen name.

- Booking an appointment with a voice training coach, or downloading a voice training app.

If you're able to manage it emotionally, you could even ask your spouse to marry you again as their true gender, with their chosen name.

Some of these things can be painful, but undertaking them doesn't just help your partner; they also provide a way for you to acknowledge and honor what came before, and to release it.

There will be new memories in the years to come, and the rites of passage you celebrate together now will be part of them.

To be yourself in a world that is constantly trying to make you something else is the greatest accomplishment.
Ralph Waldo Emerson

PUSHING BACK CAN BE HELPFUL

In the section titled *Things They'll Experience* we discussed how transgender people need to experiment with behaviors, fashion, voice, and other things to figure out how they want to manifest their gender. Style is a personal decision, and trans people can be hungry to test styles they wished they could have tried when they were younger. During this experimentation, your beloved may do or say things that leave you baffled. And while experimentation is necessary, there are times when you might need to push back. This is a thin line to walk, because testing things is necessary. Your partner may have the vulnerability of a newly emerged butterfly, stretching and flexing unfamiliar wings. Your goal should be to help steer them away from what they probably don't really want, while not damaging the fragile new beauty as it unfolds.

Transitioning people aren't children, but remembering the stages of personality shift which take place during adolescence and the teen years can be helpful. Just as people in those life phases need the freedom to test their wings, they also need loving, gentle voices to let them know when they venture out of bounds.

If your partner doesn't respond well to your feedback, perhaps they have a friend who can speak truth, gently. If there is no one else, consider finding resources online that offer advice about the issues you're finding challenging. Ask your beloved questions about who they find inspiring as a role model, and then evaluate together the various elements contributing to the persona that person manifests. Only you know what works and doesn't work when problem solving with your loved one.

Ultimately, how your partner presents gender should be completely up to them. You have the honor of helping them figure out what makes them feel the most like themselves.

It's like trans people are plopped down on an island where there is no gender, and you have to choose who you want to end up being. You develop and grow so you can eventually emerge as yourself. As an older trans person, you have the power to change the world through that establishment of male and femaleness in your own image.
Declan DeWitt Hall

CREATE TOGETHERNESS ACTIVITIES

Your transitioning loved one may be tempted to withdraw into a protective shell because the emotion can be too much to handle. You yourself may want to do the same. If you've decided to stay together through this, closing each other off can't be an option for long. Creating ways to reconnect and increase intimacy is important. Here are a few suggestions for how to do that, from people in situations like yours:

- Set aside time to do fun things and talk about anything other than transition.

- Increase touch in non-sexual ways: giving hand or foot rubs, stroking or brushing each other's hair, scratching each other's backs.

- One couple purchased a deck of cards designed to spark deep conversations about the nature of love, and they use them as a tool for opening the door for communication.

- Another couple committed to complementing each other in front of friends and family.

- For people of faith, praying together can increase intimacy.

Sometimes feeling united comes naturally and easily, other times it takes work. Transition means you both might need to put in extra effort to remain close. Making sure you have happy experiences together is an important part of maintaining the health of your relationship.

> *Do not worry that your life is turning upside down. How do you know the side you are used to is better than the one to come?*
> Rumi

GOING PUBLIC

LET YOUR LOVED ONE DRIVE

There isn't a single right or wrong way to come out to friends, family, and co-workers. Each couple faces individual circumstances that will drive decision making.

Your beloved may feel so free after telling you the news that they want to proclaim it to the world immediately. This could terrify you. Or it might feel like they're dragging their heels when you want to bite the bullet and get the whole thing over with.

But you can't decide for them. Outing a trans person is a deep and potentially dangerous violation.

Coming out is an action which unfolds over time, and results in emotional ripples and unforeseen shifts. As with pretty much all the topics related to transitioning, the pace of telling people in your lives ultimately must be the decision of your partner. You can offer insights about potential impact, but it's their existence being trapped. Hopefully they'll want to work with you to create a coming out approach that is as comfortable as possible for both of you, though that may not be the case.

So much of the transitioning process shows the strengths and weaknesses of relationships. Coming out is one of the issues that tests your communication skills and flexibility as a couple.

Trans people—trans women, especially—can find their first few steps as themselves in public particularly stressful. That stress is why it's so often important for us to have safe ways to explore who we are, under whatever veil of anonymity we can concoct for ourselves. When we're behind that veil, we can divorce ourselves from the identities we were assigned at birth, at least a little bit. To have that veil punctured is a great violence...
Emily VanDerWerff

116

CHOOSE CAREFULLY

Coming out to the public kicks off a new phase of transition, resulting in new freedoms and increased vulnerability. Because of this, it's important to choose who you come out to first very carefully. You'll both need positivity and encouragement, so it's best to come out to the safest people early on.

As you share your beloved's reality, people will talk. Consider who's likely to spill the beans when you develop your communication plan, and identify who you don't want to hurt the most so you can avoid making them feel excluded.

You and your beloved will have to navigate this territory carefully. It's an arena that can cause conflict, because your ideas of who can handle the news and who can't might differ.

There's no right method for coming out. For some people you may want to meet in person, tell others by phone, and still others by letter or text. It all depends on the individual relationships and personalities, how vulnerable your loved one feels, how likely each individual is to react in hurtful ways, and how much processing time various people need for big news.

If you'll be meeting in person with family who are likely to have difficulty, you might want to bring along supporters. People to consider include affirming clergy, representatives from a trans support group who can answer general questions, and supportive family members or friends who are known and respected by those with whom you're meeting.

As part of coming out, it's helpful to state how your loved one wants to be referred to in the future, so people know right up front and don't have to flounder. Your partner may decide some people can be exceptions to those expectations however. Perhaps an elderly grandparent or a person with cognitive difficulties who simply couldn't understand, or someone in the midst of illness or life trauma so extreme they don't have the emotional bandwidth to navigate the shift. Exempting these people is a form of grace your trans partner extends out of love, if and when they're able, for however long they're able. It isn't blanket permission to misgender. It's simply a temporary state offered out of love due to individual circumstances.

Coming out is a huge step in the transition process, and likely to be emotionally fraught. Gird your hearts and minds as you enter in. Be smart about how it unfolds. And stick together through it.

People changed lots of other personal things all the time. They dyed their hair and dieted themselves to near death. They took steroids to build muscles and got breast implants and nose jobs so they'd resemble their favorite movie stars. They changed names and majors and jobs and husbands and wives. They changed religions and political parties. They moved across the country or the world—even changed nationalities. Why was gender the one sacred thing we weren't supposed to change? Who made that rule?
Ellen Wittlinger

HELP OTHERS COPE

Whether you like it or not, you have tremendous influence with the people who love your partner. In this moment, you've been given the opportunity to be a bridge builder, peacekeeper, educator, and grace extender. This is a time to share what you yourself had to learn: that transition isn't about them, and isn't done to hurt them. This task is a burden, but it's a blessed one. It may feel like too much, and at some points in the process you might not be able to manage it and will need to create boundaries and take a break.

If you have children with your transitioning beloved, your role is particularly important. The goal of parenting should always be to raise the kids into the best possible versions of themselves. Since you've made it this far into the book, you haven't written your relationship off yet, and are trying to do your part to make things work in some configuration or other. Children will look to you to determine how they should react. Younger children may simply accept the shift with little difficulty. Older children may assess how you feel about it and mimic that response. Your kids care about you both, and will have their own complex mix of emotions, particularly if they're worried about you and your reactions.

Part of your job will be to help them not do that. Kids need people in their lives who love them. If your partner was a loving, caring presence before transition, protecting that relationship is what's best for everyone.

It can be hard to do this, particularly if things aren't going smoothly. If you're having trouble encouraging kids through the process of your partner's transition, please seek help. Remember the flight attendant wisdom: put on your own oxygen mask before attempting to help others. If you aren't functioning well, you can't do a good job of taking care of others. Counseling can help you manage the shifting world you're experiencing.

You've been given a choice: to be a bridge-builder who seeks to maintain, repair, and rebuild relationships or to destroy them. Think carefully about the kind of person you choose to be.

In a world where trans people are demeaned, excluded, exoticized, invalidated, legislated against, and killed—the courage it takes for trans people to live fully into who they are is worthy of respect and honor. I dare say it is a holy act.
Angela Yarber

DEFEND YOUR BELOVED

Things may get a bit crazy once your loved one begins to share their truth publicly. Some people will want to gauge your reaction and see how much negativity they can speak. Others may simply not care how you feel, and spew their opinions regardless of how little they actually know about transgender experience.

It's part of your job to defend them. As discussed previously, you need safe spaces to work through your own process of acceptance and change, but try not to speak unsupportively about your loved one outside that circle. Try to only say things you're willing to say in front of your partner. If the idea that they're listening makes you uncomfortable, the words you're thinking probably shouldn't be spoken.

Set boundaries, particularly for people likely to be obnoxious. If establishing boundaries has been hard for you in other contexts, it won't be easy, but it *is* going to be increasingly important.

Some people may try to say that you or your beloved are "too sensitive" about pronouns, deadnames, or other issues. Don't fall for it. Correct them calmly and consistently. Offer resources for their education.

When people behave badly, try asking why they're so invested in someone else's gender identity. How does it impact them?

Your beloved doesn't have to justify themselves, their gender, or their existence, to anyone. Other people's opinions can hurt, but they have zero impact on the reality of a person's gender. The trans person will still be trans, regardless of what anyone else says or thinks.

Defending your beloved will get easier with practice. It can be harder for those who are conflict avoidant, but you can do it. Your heart will expand through the process, and your relationship will improve because of it.

> *Trans people don't owe their cis family/loved ones time to grieve.*
> *That makes our transition, our identity, our fight for our lives, about*
> *their grief. Your grief is about you, not me. Own your grief. Don't*
> *use it as an excuse for refusing to accept me.*
> Rev. Joey Armstrong

CREATE AN ANGER MANAGEMENT PLAN

In a perfect world stepping into living gender authentically wouldn't cause upheaval, but our world is far from perfect. There's a very good chance people are going to make you both mad. Someone might out your loved one and create havoc with friends or family members. Something similar might happen at a job. Working through transition has plenty of challenges even when things are going smoothly. Adding the fuel of anger and outrage to the mix can create explosions.

Periodic anger is inevitable, so it makes sense to plan for how to respond when it hits. Your response will vary depending on the people involved. There won't be a one-size-fits-all solution, but you *can* agree to some guidelines to help minimize firestorms. For example, you could agree to wait 24 hours after the inciting event before responding, or that you'll respond in writing. You might create a few one-liner replies to shut down discussion concisely but firmly.

Different situations will require different approaches, so you'll want to think through how to handle getting mad at work, at church, with particular family members, with children, and in the other settings which comprise your life.

Anger is very likely to happen, and it may hit at times, places, and from sources that surprise you. Having a plan helps minimize the danger that you or your beloved will blow your top and further increase the disruption.

> *...being trans in this world is having to constantly justify your right to existence at all, and when you're forced to be on the defensive all the time, everything starts to look like an attack.*
> Neon Yang

YOU MIGHT LOSE RELATIONSHIPS

Choosing to stand by a transgender loved one probably means cutting ties with some people. Not everyone will be willing or able to overcome their religious training or other biases and accept your loved one's reality.

It can take time for things to shake out and for people to settle into what their responses will actually be once they receive the news. Some people may act supportive initially and then turn their backs as transition proceeds. This can happen fast or through a slow exclusion. Others may initially react badly but turn out to be fantastic allies.

Setting boundaries to protect and respect your partner is a critical task that sometimes acts as the final blow to problematic relationships. For those who aren't willing to respect your beloved's name and pronouns or who otherwise demonstrate a lack of willingness to embrace reality, it may be time to cut the strings.

There's a good chance that the relationships you lose will be a mix of those you're truly saddened to see go, and those that are a relief. Each of these determinations is unique and must be evaluated based on the characteristics of the relationship; how long they've been in place, how close you truly are, what the impact will be on others, and a variety of other factors. But the bottom line is that your beloved's health and truth need to be honored, validated, and protected. Anyone who isn't willing to do that doesn't deserve to be part of your lives.

This is hard truth, but you may be surprised to find allies springing up when and where you least expect them. "Chosen family" is often more emotionally healthy than that which comes through blood connections.

Becoming completely yourself is a good way to figure out which people in your life are pretty deeply invested in your misery.
Rev. Junia Joplin

THE BOTTOM LINE

YOUR MARRIAGE MAY NOT SURVIVE

Relationships can withstand all sorts of stressors: financial struggle, job upheaval, health crisis, even the death of a child. It can be hard on relationships when one person changes, and it's not necessarily easier when both do. Sometimes the mutual shifts fit together like cogs intersecting, and a couple's bond is strengthened. Many relationships weather the storm of transition and go on to be closer and healthier than ever before. But sometimes the relationship simply can't survive.

Your spouse may realize they partnered with you as part of their role as someone they're not. They may feel like they need to end the relationship in order to live authentically.

You yourself may decide you can't overcome the kinds of challenges transition introduces. For some situations, walking through transition with a partner is just not possible. If you conclude that's the case for you, admit it. If you've put in the work of analyzing yourself and the two of you as a couple, and are certain you can't do it, let them know. They deserve the truth.

Transitioning can be a life saver. It might be better (and safer) for a trans person to go through the process alone than having to fight you about it, or cope with ongoing pushback about accepting all the changes that are inevitable. Having to hide creates resentments that could gradually erode the good parts remaining in your relationship.

It's not fair for the person you love to have to sacrifice their authenticity to make you happy. And it's not fair for you to be miserable.

These are tough choices. But we're only given one wild and precious life. We all must decide how best to live it.

Tell me, what else should I've done?
Doesn't everything die at last, and too soon?
Tell me, what is it you plan to do
with your one wild and precious life?
Mary Oliver

YOUR MARRIAGE MAY IMPROVE SIGNIFICANTLY

A spiritual director once told me divorce rates for second and third marriages are higher than for first, because people don't unpack the baggage they've accumulated before entering a new relationship. If you and your partner carried a bunch of emotional suitcases into your coupledom, there's a good chance you'll struggle as transition unfolds.

That's not necessarily a bad thing. The struggle can motivate you to do the work together so you can be free from lingering dysfunction.

People in online groups for partners and family members of transgender people regularly report that as they've progressed down the path of the transition journey, they've never felt closer. Being your beloved's support in becoming themselves can unite you more than you ever imagined, revealing things about yourself and them that permit new freedom and openness, increased trust and intimacy, and deeper, more interconnected love.

If you're both willing and able to do the hard work, your relationship can be transformed forever. If not, there's a good chance your union won't survive.

Transition is never easy. But it doesn't have to be devastating. It can offer deep, deep blessings.

You don't got to transition. You get to. And God goes with you.
Rev. Dawn Bennett

YOU MAY REALIZE YOU'RE MORE THAN YOU KNEW

As we look back on our lives, we often find we learned the most during times of trial. Job losses, disruptions in faith communities, geographic moves, and other shifts can all seem devastating in the moment, but the rearview mirror displays ways we grew through them. A loved one coming out as transgender is similarly disruptive of normalcy.

Any time we're faced with a life challenge we're offered two paths; to shut down and find ways to unleash our hurt onto others, or to let the pain expand our compassion, deepen our self-understanding, and/or connect more fully into our faith lives. It's rare that someone immediately plunges into the second path. In fact, many of us wander along the first for some time, bewildered, upset, and angry.

Regardless of where you currently are, you have the opportunity to shift. Your soul whispers to you even now that care and compassion are there, waiting for you. Care for your beloved, and care for yourself, regardless of whether your relationship survives transition.

Trans people are forced to be the proverbial cities on a hill which act as instruction and insight to others. Their bravery creates a presence which gives others the opportunity to challenge their biases and overcome them. It's an uncomfortable role that few of us would actively seek. In your love for them, you play a similar role. You offer a glimpse to others about what love, support, and courage look like.

Your beloved is on a journey of becoming fully, beautifully, completely themselves. And so are you. Their coming out offers them the chance to do this. It offers you the same chance. Your changes may be less outwardly recognizable, but are still just as profound.

The Bottom Line

The traumas and challenges of life refine us or burn us to a crisp. The world desperately needs more people who choose to be strengthened and polished rather than becoming dark shadows.

There are two paths. You get to pick.

You're allowed to outgrow people.
This includes past versions of yourself.
Mindy Hale

CONCLUSION

Nothing stays the same. Visit the street you grew up on and you'll discover things that weren't there before and miss places that were important in your memories. Your partner both is and isn't the person they were on the day you met. Who you are right now is different from who you were yesterday, who you'll be when you take your final breath.

You've probably realized that much of what we've discussed in this book applies to couples in all sorts of circumstances. Change triggers disruption, and partners must find ways to work through that disruption. Communication is key. Generosity of spirit is needed. Mutual understanding must be sought. These are all elements of what makes a relationship healthy.

There is no escaping change, there is only choice in how we respond to the things that create it. Will we choose to be a vine that shifts direction to twine around the lattice and reach toward the sun, or one that creeps along the ground where its flowers are hidden in the grass? Will we permit the carbon atoms of our selfhood to be transformed into diamonds under pressure, or let them be crushed?

Conclusion

The world thinks it can set boundaries for who and what we are, but each of us is in charge of forming ourselves into the person we want to be. And those expectations change over time. As you continue your path into the future, you and your beloved may both discover you're stronger than you realized, and more confident in yourselves. Neither of you are likely to end up as the person you imagine being in three, five, or ten years from today, and that's okay. Life is about change and growth. Only lifeless things don't grow, and even those are altered by erosion, pressure, or entropy.

It's your time now, tomorrow, and forever.

Embrace the fullness of who you want to be as a human.

Step into your fullness.

Reach toward love, light, and hope.

APPENDIX A: FINDING A COUNSELOR

Gender-specialist Therapist Locators

National Queer & Trans Therapists of Color Network
https://nqttcn.com/en/

Psychology Today
https://www.psychologytoday.com/us/therapists/transgender

The Psychotherapist Association for Gender & Sexual Diversity
https://directory.gaylesta.org/find-a-therapist/

The World Professional Association for Transgender Health
https://www.wpath.org/provider/search

Faith-Based Counseling Organizations

The Christian Closet

https://www.thechristiancloset.com/

Progressive Christian Counseling

https://www.progressivechristiancounseling.com/

Waves Therapy for Jewish People

https://www.wavespsych.com/jewish-trans-and-jewish-queer

APPENDIX B: A RITE OF MOURNING

Yearning for a new way will not produce it. Only ending the old way can do that. You cannot hold onto the old all the while declaring that you want something new. The old will defy the new; the old will deny the new; the old will decry the new. There is only one way to bring in the new. You must make room for it.
Neale Donald Walsch

Transition is a life shift that results in a variety of things being left behind as the new future unfolds. Rites of mourning help you honor what came before and say goodbye so you're able to move forward in the healthiest way possible.

A sample morning ritual is offered below. It's agnostic in approach. If you're a person of faith, you can ask a clergy person to help you modify this one. Reading the text of the liturgy aloud helps increase your sense of participating in something external, formal, and properly honoring.

PREPARING A SPACE

Choose a spot which brings you peace. It can be inside or outside, at home, in a religious space, or anywhere that feels appropriate for the purpose. Have somewhere comfortable to sit, with a table holding a candle and something to light it with.

Gather objects representing the things you're losing, such as paperwork that include your partner's former name, clothing you loved them wearing, or a wedding photo. Give some thought to the things that bring you grief, and gather tokens representing them, for example, a picture of a family member who has rejected your beloved, or a bulletin from the church you can no longer attend.

Create a list of things you need to formally release and mourn. You'll reference these things as part of the liturgy.

135

PREPARING YOURSELF

Quiet and center yourself. A few deep breaths in through the nose and out through the mouth helps. Allow yourself to experience the presence of peace around and within you, despite all of life's chaos.

THE LITURGY

[To be read aloud.]

Today is for mourning. Mourning is sacred work.

[Light the candle.]

"In the deepest, darkest night of my wintered soul
I wrap myself in the blanket
of my sadness and grief,
pain and suffering,
doubts and concerns,
fears and questions,
and look out from my wondering eyes
toward the light that
dares to penetrate
the layers
of
blindness
that surround me."[8]

Today is for mourning. Mourning is sacred work.

---

[8] Excerpted from *Psalm for the Wintered Soul* by Cynthia Frado.

I acknowledge the breadth of my emotion: disappointment, fear, disbelief, rejection, shock, exhaustion, betrayal, loss.

Today is for mourning. Mourning is sacred work.

"To love what is alive, we must accept having to lose what we've made precious through our care. To be fully and fiercely human, we must accept having to be breakable and sometimes broken."[9]

Today is for mourning. Mourning is sacred work.

I celebrate the beauty inherent in things which used to be, despite their brokenness.

Today is for mourning. Mourning is sacred work.

In order to make room for what is new, I must let go of many things:

I release the name [INSERT YOUR PARTNER'S BIRTHNAME].

I release the idea of [INSERT YOUR PARTNER'S CHOSEN NAME] as anything other than their authentic gender.

I release the image of life as I'd envisioned.

I release the need to control things which I cannot.

I release my idea of family.

I release friends who have turned away.

---

[9] Greg Ward

Rite of Mourning

I release communities that have excluded my loved one or I.

I release family members who can't or won't accept what is happening.

I release expectations for what my sex life is supposed to look like.

I release [INSERT OTHER THINGS THAT NEED TO BE RELEASED].

Today is for mourning. Mourning is sacred work.

There is grief in the process of releasing, but through that grief, light glimmers.

I embrace memories of love and laughter.

I embrace my flawed and beautiful self.

I embrace the knowledge that spring always comes.

I embrace the assurance that love is real.

I embrace the reality that the future holds good things.

Today is for mourning. Mourning is sacred work.

May my sorrow lead me to unexpected places.

May empty spaces be filled with new life.

May grief create room for compassion, patience, and understanding.

May I find meaning in the confusion.

May I be transformed by grief into something new, something better, something whole.

May I have the courage to keep going.

[Extinguish the candle.]

Today is for mourning. Mourning is sacred work.

"I was never meant to remain
in this confinement of darkness.
I was created to dwell
in the infinite light.
Spring will come again,
and I will be ready for my emergence and unfolding,
that I might soar
ever higher
into my own becoming,
into the light of my own transcendence.
Reawakened.
Renewed.
Reborn."[10]

Today is for mourning. Mourning is sacred work.

ONCE THE RITE HAS CONCLUDED

Once the ritual is complete, put the items you gathered in a special memorial box if they're things that must be retained, or dispose of them, preferably in a symbolic way (by burning or burying, for example) if they don't need to be kept.

---

[10] Excerpted from *Psalm for the Wintered Soul* by Cynthia Frado.

APPENDIX C: RESOURCES FOR FURTHER STUDY AND SUPPORT

Crisis Resources

24-Hour Crisis Text Line: www.crisistextline.org, or text HOME to 741741 to connect to a crisis counselor, in English or Spanish.

Trans Lifeline: www.translifeline.org, or call 877-565-8860 in the United States, or 877-330-6366 in Canada.

Suicide Prevention Lifeline: www.suicidepreventionlifeline.org, or call 1-800-273-8255 for English, or 1-888-628-9454 for Spanish.

Resources for Partners of Transgender People

The Reflective Workbook for Partners of Transgender People by D.M. Maynard, Jessica Kingsley Publishers, 2019.

The Trans Partner Handbook: A Guide for When Your Partner Transitions by Jo Green, Jessica Kingsley Publishers, 2017

Transgender Partners resource list:
https://www.transgenderpartners.com/resource-for-partners-2

Love Is Respect partner support overview:
https://www.loveisrespect.org/resources/supporting-your-partner-through-transition/

Gender Education Resources

www.MyProunouns.org

www.GenderSpectrum.org

https://www.thetrevorproject.org/resources/article/understanding-gender-identities/

Fox Fisher's YouTube Channel:
https://www.youtube.com/foxandowl

Resources for Adjusting to Change

Who Moved My Cheese by Dr. Spencer Johnson, G.P. Putnam's Sons, 1998.

The Power of Letting Go, John Purkiss, Aster, 2020.

INDEX